THE
DEAN FOREST
RAILWAY

·A PAST and PRESENT COMPANION·

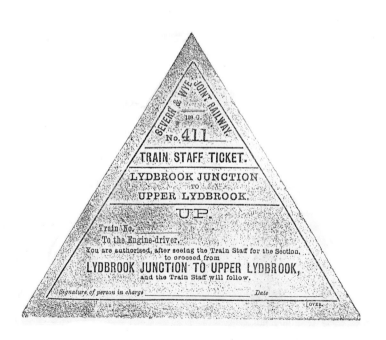

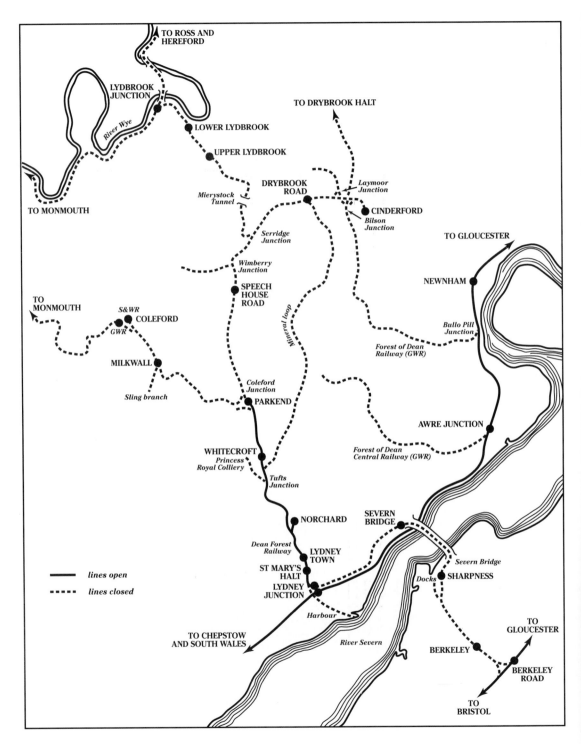

Map of the Dean Forest Railway and associated lines

THE
DEAN FOREST
RAILWAY

·A PAST and PRESENT COMPANION·

A nostalgic trip along the former Severn & Wye lines from Lydney to Parkend, Coleford, Cinderford and Lydbrook

John Stretton

S. W. 213.

SEVERN & WYE JOINT RAILWAY
(G. W. & Mid.).

PASSENGERS' LUGGAGE.

To CARDIFF.

·RAILWAY HERITAGE·
from
The NOSTALGIA *Collection*

First published in 2002
Reprinted 2006

British Library Cataloguing in Publication Data

A catalogue record for this book is available from the British Library.

ISBN 1 85895 206 9
ISBN 978 1 85895 206 2

Past & Present Publishing Ltd
The Trundle
Ringstead Road
Great Addington
Kettering
Northants NN14 4BW

Tel/Fax: 01536 330588
email: sales@nostalgiacollection.com
Website: www.nostalgiacollection.com

Printed and bound in Great Britain

Past and Present

A Past & Present book
from
The NOSTALGIA Collection

ACKNOWLEDGEMENTS

As with any project of this nature, it has been collaboration. In other words, many people have been involved, giving advice and/or practical assistance. Contributions have varied, some major, others less so, but all have been greatly appreciated and this book would have been the poorer without them. There are too many to mention all by name, but especial thanks must go to Hugh Ballantyne, Eric Bareham, Rod Blencowe, Colin Caddy, Richard Casserley, Paul Chancellor, Maurice Dart, John Edgington, Mike Esau, Tom Heavyside, Frank Hornby, David Hughes, Colin Jacks, Keith Johnson, David Johnson at Millbrook House Ltd, Brian Miller, National Monuments Record office in Swindon, Graham Stacey, Frank Robertshaw, Graham Roose, Peter Treloar, Bob Tuck, Adrian Vaughan, John White, Edwin Wilmshurst, Tony Wright and especially Fergie Scoon. In addition, I am grateful to Geoff Silcock for allowing me to capture the front cover shot during one of his charters. Peter, Mick and Will at Silver Link Publishing have been as accommodating, encouraging and patient as ever; as have my wife and daughter, Judi and Tammy, who have supported and encouraged me, and provided valuable company and assistance on trips to the Forest – I will try to remember to load film into the camera next time! Thank you all!

CONTENTS

This picture, so full of character, could so easily have been from any number of GWR branches, but depicted here is the real beginning of the ex-Severn & Wye incursion into the Forest of Dean. On a rather dull 29 July 1950, ex-GWR 0-6-0PT No 2080 heads away from Lydney Junction station, past the engine shed (right) on the last stretch of its journey with a Berkeley Road-Lydney Town service. A member of Dean's 140-strong '2021' Class, designed with 4ft 1½in driving wheels, No 2080 emerged from Swindon Works in 1900, originally built as a saddle tank. Shedded at Lydney at nationalisation in 1948, it here wears the 85B shedplate of Gloucester (Horton Road), the parent depot of Lydney, from where it was withdrawn on 31 March 1952. Note the delightful grounded coach body, provided in 1921 as accommodation for shedmen and cleaners, the pitched roof design and condition of the repair shop buildings, the rather tall ladder leaning against the roof, the point rodding in the foreground and all manner of other details that have been swept away in succeeding years of progress on our railways. *Millbrook House collection*

INTRODUCTION

The Forest of Dean is a mysterious, magical and even mystical place. It has been so for centuries, and hopefully will remain so in the future. A wonderful place for a railway!

The Forest sits like a huge V-shaped wedge between the rivers Wye and Severn, with the majority of the area sitting above substantial coal measures. Although the iron-ore around the edges of this area was certainly worked by the Romans, 'industrialisation' came late to the Forest, as it was a royal hunting ground with the lands belonging to the Crown as early as the Domesday Book. The birth of the Severn & Wye Railway arose from the particular geological composition of the Forest and the need to find ways of capitalising on this and its by-products. Specifically, the roots of the railway lay in the arrival and proliferation of tramways in the early years of the 19th century.

The idea of linking these two river courses by a horse-drawn tramroad was first mooted in 1799 by traders of Hereford and Gloucester in search of cheaper coal. An Act of Parliament of 10 June 1809 established the 'Lydney and Lidbrook Railway' (sic), which opened in 1810 as a 3ft 6in gauge line, but this was altered in 1811 to 'The Severn and Wye Railway and Canal Company', authorising the construction of a canal and harbour at Lydney. With the coming of the South Wales Railway's extension from Chepstow to Gloucester in 1851, and the provision of interchange facilities at Lydney, pressure was on to convert to a proper railway. Various proposals were made as to the best way forward, especially bearing in mind several competing schemes, but relatively little was done other than ordering five locomotives for the tramroad in 1864/5. By 1867, however, it was obvious that the tramroad was inadequate to cope with increasing traffic and customer demands.

Thus in 1868 the Severn & Wye Railway came to construct a broad gauge (7ft 0¼in) line alongside the tramroad from Lydney northwards into the Forest, followed by a Mineral Loop from Tufts Junction in 1869. A link from Serridge Junction to the Ross & Monmouth Railway at Lydbrook came in 1874. Much of this was driven by demands for smoother and faster shipment/transhipment of the mineral wealth of the area. Conversion to standard gauge came in 1872, with a new locomotive being added to the stock in addition to the conversion of the existing five broad gauge engines, and passenger services began in 1875.

In 1879 the basic layout into the Forest was 'extended outwards' by an Act of Parliament of 21 July of that year. Authorising the construction of a bridge over the River Severn, a line was constructed from Lydney over the bridge to Sharpness and Berkeley Road on the existing Midland Railway line from Birmingham to Bristol. Initially separate from the S&W, the two quickly amalgamated, changing the name to Severn & Wye & Severn Bridge Railway. This gave the railway an independent outlet to markets in the UK, rather than suffering the constraints placed on it by its competitor, the GWR, at Lydney Junction. Thereafter, fortunes on the Severn & Wye fluctuated like many another early railway operation, and in 1894, in financial straits after depression in the Forest, the MR and GWR jointly took over the operation of the railway, although little actually changed from the services previously run by the S&WR.

As will be seen in the Gazetteer, this extension was brutally curtailed one dark night on 25 October 1960 when the Severn Bridge was 'rammed' by two out-of-control barges en route to Sharpness, dumping two spans into the rushing waters below! The arrival of motor buses, improving road connections, and competing rail links all took their own toll, with the ex-S&WR system suffering passenger withdrawal in 1929 and final closure to freight in 1976. The last freight ran on 7 May of that year, when diesel-electric locomotive No 37270 cleared the last remaining wagons from Parkend Sidings and transferred them to Lydney yard.

Thankfully, this date was sufficiently late to enable the emerging Dean Forest Railway preservation movement to mobilise support and finance to keep alive the sights and sounds of railway operation in the Forest.

This book is not intended to be a definitive history and/or appreciation of the ex-S&WR. That job has been done much more eloquently and in far greater detail by others – especially the wonderful 'trilogy' produced many years ago by publisher Wild Swan and now sadly out of print. Similarly, I am aware that I have merely scratched the surface of the preservation movement. This is partly due to space, but is also a deliberate ploy: I have merely attempted to show some of what there was/is and hope to encourage others to both visit the 'new' railway, based at Norchard, and to savour the delights of the Forest itself. There will be photographs – especially the older ones – that will be familiar to some, but I have attempted wherever possible to search out images that have not been previously published. I hope they provide pleasure and some surprises.

Of all the books I have produced so far, this was certainly one of the most enjoyable on which to work, not only for the superb and evocative 'past' photographs, but also the ready help from so many, the sheer joy of touring the Forest, spotting tell-tale signs of the old railway, trying to imagine what it must have been like, and simply soaking in the atmosphere. I hope readers will experience some of the wonder for themselves.

Originally constructed to Brunel's broad gauge, the Severn & Wye Railway was converted to the smaller 'standard' gauge in 1872. Rolling-stock was altered as quickly as possible including, among other items, the first of these two locomotives. The elder of the two, *Friar Tuck* (Avonside 810/1870), arrived on the railway in December 1870 and is seen in the upper picture at an unidentified location on the S&W, late in Queen Victoria's reign, proudly displaying a delightfully designed and executed lining. Eventually becoming MR No 1122A after transfer to that railway in 1895, then No 1605, the locomotive was eventually scrapped from Derby in 1911.

In contrast, *Will Scarlet*, although of very similar design, was built by Fletcher Jennings & Co in November 1873 (Works No 122). Sold exactly 39 years later to Bute Works Supply, in South Wales, it was eventually returned to capital stock, but to the GWR this time on the Alexandra Dock Railway, as No 32. Later renumbered 1356, it remained in service until 1921, eventually being cut up in September 1923. *Robin Hood* and *Little John* also worked on the S&WR – what was the connection between the Dean and Sherwood Forests? *Both Peter Treloar collection*

Lydney Junction

The point where many travellers intending to visit the Forest of Dean would make their connection was Lydney Junction. Here just named 'Lydney', but with the added epithet 'for the Severn & Wye Joint Railway', the ex-South Wales Railway Lydney Junction station was a busy place, situated on the Gloucester-South Wales main line that skirted the western shore of the River Severn. It is seen here in the early 1960s – witness the parcels trolleys on both platforms, the bike against the main station building, the toilet block, two figures on the up platform, just past the water tower, and the healthily loaded siding in the distance, to the right of one of the wagon repair shops.

By the time of the preparation of this book, the station looked very different – a couple of basic waiting shelters and little else – but at least still open for business. By the road level crossing that formerly shared space with a mineral line to the dock, this 1932 Rights of Way Act sign was still proudly displaying. *Lens of Sutton/MJS*

Above For passengers making the connection between the GWR and S&WR, a long latticework iron footbridge was provided in 1908, straddling the exchange sidings occupying the land between the two railways. This is the view that would be seen when heading for the S&WR station, looking towards the Forest and the town of Lydney. The branch station is on the extreme right, with Lydney Engine Shed signal box seen beyond and the town's church spire beyond that. On 12 April 1964 an unidentified pannier tank shunts on the line that led to the docks, while in the centre of the picture the yard shunter chats to a colleague. Note the twin water tanks of the engine shed, seen in the picture on page 6, just above the pannier's trailing smoke. *F. A. Blencowe, R. K. Blencowe collection*

Below The route of the S&WR into and through the Forest was administered jointly by the Great Western and Midland companies with effect from 1 July 1894. Evidence of that is seen here, in this view from the up platform of the ex-S&WR station on 23 September 1950, with the connection to the main line and the run to the Severn Bridge curving away to the left. *H. C. Casserley, Richard Casserley collection*

The long footbridge mentioned opposite can be seen here descending to make connection with the S&WR station. This time the station sign, vintage 1898, does pronounce the location as a Junction and advising 'Change for South Wales, Paddington & Great Western Line'. The Midland Railway influence can also be seen in the 'Hawkseye' lozenge-style sign and fencing next to the rather unusual station building. Originally a much smaller affair designed by William Eassie, the structure was expanded by the Gloucester Wagon Co, providing all necessary amenities and topped off by Countess slates and ornamental ridge tiling. Pictured in July 1950, the station boasts two members of staff, seating and hoardings, but evidence that things are not what they used to be can be found in the white edging to the platform, which only extends to a point level with the building, with grass beginning to take a hold at the left-hand edge of this view and on the up platform opposite. Plainly, shorter trains are now the norm, a point proved to some degree by the tantalising glimpse of an ex-GWR railcar on the extreme right just departing for Lydney Town.

In August 2001, 51 years later, the picture is very different. Gone are the bridge, the up platform and the tall chimneys beyond, but at least there is still a railway! Now in the hands of the preservationists, Lydney Junction is gradually coming back to life, with a new waiting shelter in roughly the position of the old and a superb recreation of the original station sign, lovingly designed by railway volunteer and servant David Hughes. A lone passenger looks for information of the next service. *Roger Carpenter collection/MJS*

This is the same general view, but swapping platforms. In an undated view, probably from the early years of the 20th century, the up platform is graced by a standard Gloucester Wagon Co shelter and adorned by gas lamps and a delightful array of advertising hoardings. The joint GW and MR administration is reflected in posters for GWR travel and an advert for 'MR Hotels', in particular Manchester's 'New Midland Hotel ... One of the Finest Hotels in Europe'!

In August 2001 the change is more dramatic. Now there is no up platform at all, and it is hard to visualise one ever having been there. The signal box to serve both the restored railway and the road crossing stands on virtually the same spot as of yore, but elsewhere the surrounding hinterland has undergone much evolution. *Lens of Sutton/MJS*

On the same platforms, but this time looking eastwards towards the main line, the 'lozenge' station sign and fencing again betray the MR influence, as the site enjoys a siesta awaiting the arrival of the next train.

The new waiting shelter is again visible, with, beyond, the telegraph pole having moved sides and, on the left, all sign of the old platform obliterated. *Lens of Sutton/MJS*

On 15 April 1956 the Railways Enthusiasts' Club ran 'The Severn Venturer', a special train to South Gloucestershire and the Forest of Dean lines. Hauled throughout by No 1625, the train is here seen taking water at Lydney Junction prior to continuing the journey into the Forest. In the days of 'auto-trains' between Berkeley Road and Lydney Town, this water column was important, as there was no similar facility on the up platform here, nor any supply at Town station. New in August 1950, No 1625 became a casualty of the post-1955 Modernisation Plan, being withdrawn from Hereford shed less than ten years later, on 18 June 1960.

Preparing to make a return journey to Norchard, No 9642, built in 1946 and now enjoying a rebirth on the DFR after withdrawal from BR in 1964, stands with its train on 30 April 2000. There is no water tower here yet and little else, but evidence of continuing work at the site can be had from the plastic protective fencing on the platform. *Hugh Ballantyne/MJS*

As stated earlier, latter-day BR services were handled by short trains; indeed, some were only graced with single-car diesel railcars. Introduced by the GWR in an attempt to cut costs and help ailing branches/services survive, the units were the forerunners of what became a similar exercise under the 1955 Modernisation Plan and went on to spawn the ubiquitous DMUs seen everywhere on our rail network at the close of the 20th century. On a decidedly gloomy-looking 22 July 1950, No W7 waits to make the run on to Lydney Town with a Birmingham Locomotive Club railtour. Although wearing a tail lamp, it is interesting to note the presence of two crew in the cab and the driver's door open. Note the hoarding board on the left emblazoned 'London Midland & Scottish Railway' – no mention of joint administration there! The fencing to the left led to the footbridge ramp.

In 2001, on an equally gloomy day, the station still has a starter signal, though positioned slightly further away from the tracks, and a signal box. The station sign on the left recreates the 'lozenge' style. *R. K. Blencowe collection/MJS*

Above In a wonderful scene, full of character, auto-tank No 1430 is replenished with water by the fireman on 24 July 1958. Before the final run to Lydney Town, the driver takes a moment away from the footplate to look somewhat suspiciously along the platform, his expression seeming to indicate that he is not wholly happy with something! His work-stained over-trousers do not quite cover his own trousers and look as though they could slip down at any moment; the open-neck shirt, bulging jacket pocket and flat cap complete the picture. The fireman has one eye on the water pipe and the other on his 'gaffer'! Though definitely looking the part, No 1430 would only see a few more weeks of work, being withdrawn on 6 September 1958. *Gerald Adams*

Above right As one travelled between Lydney Junction and Town stations, the engine shed was passed immediately on the left, and access was controlled by Lydney Engine Shed signal box. Seen here in May 1964, it clearly displays its Midland origins, having been built in 1918 by that company, which was responsible for signalling on this section. It housed 27 levers and also controlled access to the goods yard and the Tinplate Works siding. It closed in October 1967. *R. K. Blencowe*

Right The box is again seen on the same day as No 9620 prepares to back on to the shed, having completed its immediate tasks. On this occasion the shed yard and building look bereft of life, having been closed as an operational facility two months earlier, just short of the site's centenary. It had ceased to be a full-blown depot in 1935, becoming a sub-shed to Gloucester (Horton Road). No 9620 would also soon expire, being withdrawn on 20 July. *R. K. Blencowe*

17

Above Throughout its life, Lydney's 1876 three-road shed extension was home to small tanks, with anything larger than an 0-6-0 being a rarity. In an undated view, but probably around 1950, an almost 'little and large' pairing sits in front of the shed building. No 2131 (right), a long-term resident of Lydney, has seen its best years, being withdrawn in November 1951, replaced by more modern stock. Built in 1903, at Wolverhampton, and one of Dean's '2021' Class, it was originally a saddle tank with a domeless boiler. Initially a class of 140, an impressive 120 were still in service at nationalisation. However, its companion, No 1404, is a comparative newcomer to the branch, having only been recently moved to Gloucester (Horton Road) shed from Hereford. Note the evidence of sliding doors to the shed – these needed frequent repair after loco contact! *Maurice Dart collection*

Below Two of the more modern varieties mentioned above can be seen on shed on 20 April 1958. No 1623 is of a class introduced in 1950, but was a direct descendant of the '2021' Class seen above, whereas No 7723, behind, is of older vintage, built by Kerr Stuart & Co Ltd in 1930. Note that the front of the right-hand building has had a new corrugated asbestos roof, the chimneys have lost their caps, and the chimney of the middle building has disappeared altogether. *R. O. Tuck*

Travelling further on towards Town station, the impressive tower of St Mary's Church is an eye-catching backdrop to another ancient pannier tank. From the gentle exhaust, No 2025 is obviously not in a hurry, joining the 'mineral' line from the siding by the 1869 weighing machine keeper's 'cottage'. This line ran through from Lydney Town and was used by mineral trains to run over the weighbridge. It was initially situated immediately to the right of the brake-van, but was moved circa 1889 to the loop line from which this train is emerging. Shunting duties have presumably been completed, judging by the happy smiles on the faces of what look to be shunter and fireman.

The view in April 2000 is barely recognisable, with only the church spire pinpointing the location. No 9642 slows for the tablet exchange at Junction signal box, having just crossed the level crossing over the 'new' A48 Lydney Bypass. This crossing, carving across the ex-railway land by the cottage, is the reason for the speed restriction and warning sign seen to the left of No 9642, and one of the more serious considerations for the Dean Forest Railway in these days of the Health & Safety Executive.
Millbrook House collection/MJS

The time has now moved forward to 18 September 1967 and D6320 slowly makes its way towards the ex-S&WR yards at Junction station, passing the weighbridge cottage with a mixed ballast and coal freight train from Parkend. Note how, compared with the view of No 2025 on the previous page, there has been drastic track rationalisation. The up line on the left has gone, as has the old weighbridge long loop; the track past the old Engine Shed signal box is now single; and the track into the depot has been lifted, although the shed buildings are still intact three years after closure. The foot crossing, seen just past the shunter walking alongside the tracks, is at the point where the bypass now crosses the line.

With the re-opening of the line under the aegis of the Dean Forest Railway, a new Halt has been opened at this point, originally called 'Lakeside', recognising the adjacent boating lake, but since re-named 'St Mary's Halt', acknowledging the proximity of the church and the footpath leading to it over the railway. As seen on a wet day in April 2000, yet more track re-organisation has taken place and the bypass can be clearly seen in the middle distance. Note that the cottage has been re-roofed. *Both R. K. Blencowe*

Turning through 180 degrees from the last pairing, we see D6320 again on its journey from Parkend. In former times this train would have been running 'wrong line', but with the track rationalisation already seen this is now the 'through' route. Note the site of the weighbridge loop on the left, where a box now lies discarded. Built by the North British Locomotive Co in March 1960 as part of the Modernisation Plan, D6320 first saw service giving assistance over the stiff Devon banks, but by the time of this view it had recently been moved north to Bristol (Bath Road) shed. Sadly it fell victim to a BR policy of concentrating on diesel-electric traction, so this diesel-hydraulic loco was withdrawn in May 1971 and cut up at Swindon Works a year later.

Again barely recognisable as the same place, only the curve of the track gives a clue in April 2000. Seen from the footbridge over the tracks at St Mary's Halt, the lengthy platform is to accommodate the longer trains seen in preservation, while Pidcock's Canal, which predates both tramway and railway, passes beneath. *Both R. K. Blencowe*

Lydney Town

Left and right Between Engine Shed Junction and Lydney Town station, the line runs past Bathurst Park, the wall of which can just be seen to the left of this view looking towards the throat of Town station yard and the approach to the station itself. Seen on an overcast 5 March 1958 (taken on Ilford HP3 film with an exposure of 100th second at f8), the rather ancient wooden-posted stop signal is at danger. Note that it is sited on the 'wrong' side of the tracks, because the left-hand curve around the park restricts the sight of the approach to the yard and potential conflicting movements. As well as the two through tracks, there are three access sidings to goods premises on the left, with a train of box vans being unloaded in the Hill Street yard, just to the right of the white wooden-ended building in the left middle-distance, formerly stables and latterly stores.

With the growth of trees and encroachment of undergrowth on the original trackbed, it is hardly credible that this is same place, but this is indeed the view in 2000. Gone are all the sidings, with the present line squeezing its way between the Fire Station and a retail development and offices. *R. O. Tuck/MJS*

Below In earlier times the view from the park was open, as seen in this view of April 1965 as No 8745, running bunker-first as engines inevitably did in the up direction, skirts the area with a ballast train. A member of the very large '5700' Class of 0-6-0PTs, No 8745 was built by W. G. Bagnall Ltd in 1931. A long-time resident of Yeovil shed, at the time of this shot it was almost exactly halfway through its sojourn at Gloucester, from where it was withdrawn on 19 September 1965. Judging by the relaxed mood of the fireman, the train of ex-Whitecliffe Quarry loaded hoppers is making a casual pace to Lydney Junction. *R. K. Blencowe*

Having swung left to approach the station, the line then reversed to curve right through the platforms, as seen in this view from the early years of the 20th century. With the paraphernalia of milk churns, barrow with wicker basket, gas lamps and station decoration, the site has an air of solidity and confidence. The up platform is graced with another William Eassie wooden building, whereas the down side has a far more substantial red-brick affair, complete with waiting rooms and toilets for both sexes, provided in 1897 after complaints from locals about previous facilities. Resignalling and line re-arrangement at the north end of the station also occurred at the same time, improving the alignment and the position of the singling of the track immediately past the crossing gates. A new signal box, controlling the gates as well as the trains, with a total of 31 levers, was also installed during this work.

By comparison, the scene on 30 April 1964 (*above right*) is very different. The lamps still look to be gas and the buildings are largely intact, including the substantial once-rail-served brick brewery store to the right, but having been closed to passengers following the damage to the Severn Bridge, the grass and weeds are staking their claim to the platform surfaces, and there is a lack of seating and large station signs.

Exactly 36 years later, on 30 April 2000 (*right*), the railway has closed and re-opened, but in different hands and under wholly altered circumstances. Gone is the down platform, the area now being occupied by the town's Fire Station; gone, too, are the buildings on the up platform, which itself is completely new in this view, and there is only space for a single track to maintain a railway presence. Happily, however, the Dean Forest Railway is developing and expanding its influence, both in the immediate vicinity and the wider railway world. *MJS collection/F. A. Blencowe, R. K. Blencowe collection/MJS*

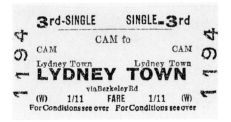

For much of its existence, the ex-S&WR system owed its livelihood to freight. Goods and produce travelled both into and out of the Forest, with coal, timber and stone especially being important commodities. In an undated view, but probably around 1950, what appears to be a low summer sun lights the side of No 2151 and its load of (predominantly) coal wagons as it heads for Lydney Junction. The first two wagons bear the owner's name of 'E. Jarrett & Co Ltd' of Bream. One of the last batch of '2021' Class locomotives, built in 1904, No 2151 spent some time in mid-Wales at Machynlleth shed, but when withdrawn in June 1952 it was allocated to Danygraig in South Wales.

In the latter years of BR's operation, passenger services were largely handled by push-pull 'auto-trains', although the practice had started earlier in GWR days. On 5 July 1947, in the year prior to nationalisation, push-pull coach A33 trailer No 4350 with the tell-tale driver's window clearly visible, waits ready for a return trip to Berkeley Road. The other coach on this day (out of sight) was A34 trailer No 1671. Note the LMS-style 'lozenge' station sign, 24 years after the Midland Railway had ceased to be!

Nearly 20 years on, in the third picture, the scene is very different. Passenger services no longer run and freight is now restricted to just a single track as D9555 heads its train of two 16T mineral wagons and brake-van through Town station on 8 August 1966, heading for Lydney Junction and the main line. Note that the signal box is still open, to control the A48 level crossing, but elsewhere, the station site is showing a distinct aura of abandonment. The last of the class to be built, in October 1965, D9555 was overtaken by the rapidly changing scene on BR and became 'surplus to requirements' in April 1969. Happily, it is now preserved at the Rutland Railway Museum.

Once more the 'present' view of the same site shows little that is recognisable. On 30 April 2000 the rear coach of a Lydney Junction-Norchard service recedes towards the road crossing, not yet stopping at the single platform, this 'new' Town station not being opened until 22 April 2001. *Maurice Dart collection/H. C. Casserley/R. K. Blencowe/MJS*

Opposite This is the view from Hill Street level crossing on 22 July 1950, as No 2080 and ex-GWR railcar W7 represent the two styles of passenger comfort in the latter years of such services. The former has arrived from Berkeley Road, run over the level crossing and reversed into the up platform, awaiting the road to return, whereas the railcar prepares to journey further into the Forest, with the Birmingham Locomotive Club special charter already seen. Yet another member of the '2021' Class to serve on the route, No 2080 was finally withdrawn in March 1953. To the left of the locomotive can be seen another Eassie-designed 'Gloucester' building, thought to have been a former signal box, but here in use in earlier times as a railway agent's office.

The scene in April 2000 shows just how much has changed over the years and how much of the delightful original architecture and ambience has been lost. No matter what efforts the present preservationists exert, there is just no way that they can successfully recreate those former visions; no thanks, of course, to the brutal encroachment on the railway from both sides. *R. K. Blencowe collection/MJS*

Above Stepping to the other side of the tracks, we see No 2025 arriving from Berkeley Road. Although undated, the view is certainly earlier than that of No 2080 opposite; the starter signal here still has a MR wooden post and original oil reservoir, whereas the later view shows the post to be LMS metal and to have moved a foot or so away from the trackside. No 2025 was one of the very first batch of '2021s', emerging from Wolverhampton Works in 1897, but it outlasted its sister No 2080 by just over two months. *R. K. Blencowe* collection

Above Having seen the passenger footbridge over the tracks by the road crossing in previous shots, the view here is from that bridge. On a dull and once more undated occasion, but certainly post-1933, the station still boasts the early station signs and notice boards headed variously 'LMS', 'Great Western Railway' and 'Severn & Wye Railway'. Gone is the proliferation of such items as milk churns, etc, seen in an earlier view, but the goods trade is still obviously healthy, as yet another '2021' pannier tank shunts a train of over a dozen wagons and vans into the Hill Street goods yard siding. The bridge was removed around 1963. *Crown copyright, NMR*

Opposite Swinging round 180 degrees from the previous views, the onwards journey towards Parkend is seen from the other side of the A48 road, with the double track through the platform very quickly becoming single. On 24 July 1964 No 3775 slows for the crossing with its load of coal empties, ballast and produce. Immediately in front of the train can be seen the beginnings of the turn-out to the old coal and timber wharf, once occupied by the Lydney Coal Co. Once again running bunker-first – virtually all locomotives had travelled into the Forest boiler-first since the earliest days – No 3775 was of 1938 vintage, built at Swindon and finally withdrawn on 15 January 1966.

Into the new century the track still clings to the same alignment and even the metal railings remain. Otherwise, once more, the scene is very different, with the coal and timber sidings having been removed around 1974. *F. A. Blencowe, R. K. Blencowe collection/MJS*

31

Leaving the environs of Lydney, the line passes as area known as Middle Forge as it heads towards the Forest. Named (with neighbouring Upper Forge) after the forges that were constructed in the early 17th century to make and work iron, the site saw many changes of use and fortune over the years, eventually reverting to forging and finally closing in 1891. Once running through open country, as seen here, with the housing on the northern extremities of Lydney on the right, the present line is now bounded by the unrestricted growth of trees and vegetation. Around 1966 D9502 displays once more the wealth of freight material that helped to keep the route alive for so long after the withdrawal of passenger services, with another ex-Whitecliffe Quarry load of ballast destined for some part of the Western Region. *R. K. Blencowe*

Norchard and Whitecroft

Above A 'bread and butter' train for the branch: with a load of well-stocked wooden-bodied and steel coal wagons, together with the appropriate headlamp code for a 'pick-up or branch freight, mineral or ballast train', No 9619 passes Norchard, near the site of the present base for the Dean Forest Railway, in January 1965, running downhill towards Town station. Whereas most locomotives used on the branch had been allocated to Gloucester, Severn Tunnel Junction shed took over responsibility after the closure of Lydney shed in 1964. No 9619 was not long for this world, being withdrawn seven months later on 8 August. *R. K. Blencowe*

Below Nearly three years later, the base now occupied by the DFR can be seen in the background in its former condition. On 29 December 1967 D6320 passes with a Coleford-Lydney working on what will become in due time the main running line up to Parkend. At the time of writing, operations are situated on the flat area just above the diesel, once the site of New Mills then Norchard Colliery. The building immediately to the right of the train is the old level entrance. Again, evidence of the value of quarrying to the line can be judged from this train. *R. K. Blencowe*

Above Yet more hard core! On 28 March 1966 D9502 drifts down the gradient towards Norchard from Tufts Junction, around 2½ miles from the main line, with its payload of 17 well-filled hopper wagons. Again the area has an open aspect, compared to subsequent years, although the DFR DMU group is making great strides in regaining the situation. D9502 was another of the short-lived (on BR) class known affectionately to enthusiasts as 'Teddy Bears'. Built in July 1964 at Swindon and allocated to Bristol (Bath Road), it was withdrawn in April 1969, with less than five years' wear, a victim of the railway's changing fortunes. *R. K. Blencowe*

Opposite Inaccessible by road, Tufts Junction was the divergence point for the Oakwood branch, leading to Princess Royal Colliery. The branch can be seen swinging left, just past the signal box, in 1964; it brought much business to the S&WR and its successors, closing, with the ending of the Colliery, in 1965. With the inevitable shunting required at the junction, the area was well supplied with sidings and crossovers, controlled by a complete set of MR semaphore signals. On the extreme left is the old 'down main', here used as a siding; next is the former up line, but now the single through route; while the track on the right was the former mineral loop. On the extreme right is the 1889-vintage signalman's cottage, like that at Lydney Junction a fairly substantial building for its role.

The view in 2000 is given away by the general line of trees in the distance and the fact that the old branch gate still clings (literally!) to its position, just past the derelict building in the middle distance. The original signal box here closed on 2 October 1967 and was subsequently demolished. Although of GWR design, it contained MR block instruments; these are now in the Science Museum in London. The MR-style box seen here came from Pirton Sidings, between Ashchurch and Abbotswood Junction, and the derelict building was intact when recovered from Barnwood Sidings in Gloucester, but has suffered from the hands of vandals. Both structures are stored here, pending use elsewhere on the DFR in due course. *R. K. Blencowe/MJS*

Seen from the 1896 standard GWR signal box seen on the previous page in 1964, No 4698 approaches with a Coleford-Lydney Junction yard freight of more railway ballast and coal empties on 24 April 1964. The Oakwood branch is seen curving to the left. Two-thirds of the way along the train the line is passing over Tufts Bridge, spanning Cannop Brook. Though no great problem during BR's time, it has proved something of an Achilles' heel for the preservationists, causing major delays in regaining the route to Parkend. Note that the road nearby can clearly be seen in this shot, a view impossible in later years.

With no signal box available, the 'present' view can only be had from the ground. The bridge can be seen just to the left of the telegraph pole, the right-hand parapet standing proud. It had been hoped to have the railway open to Parkend by 2000, but the remedial works necessary on the bridge proved to be greater and more problematic and the solutions more intractable than originally thought, inevitably delaying permission for normal service trains to run over it. *R. K. Blencowe/MJS*

Whitecroft station was a little over 3 miles from Lydney, and this is the view looking south from the road crossing on 30 December 1963, as pannier tank No 1650, wreathed in steam, restarts its short freight to continue its journey to Lydney Junction. Although the gates of the Whitecroft Pin Manufacturing Co are closed – presumably for the New Year period – the smoking chimney behind and the general demeanour of the station all give the impression of an active railway. Note the instantly recognisable William Eassie-designed station building, from the near end to the downpipe, with a sympathetic extension added in 1899. By this date the station has lost its lighting, nameboard and seating, but has gained MR-style fencing on the left in place of the original plainer wooden one.

The factory buildings and old fence post on the left remain and the tracks have been relaid by the DFR, with the exception of the siding, but otherwise the railway has succumbed to 'progress' in April 2000. *F. A. Blencowe, R. K. Blencowe collection/MJS*

This is the station as seen from the south. On 15 April 1956 an enthusiasts' special has come to a halt in the platform, on its way towards the deeper parts of the Forest, allowing passengers to enjoy the delights of this small country station. The siding to the left, complete with the 1890 Gloucester Wagon Co goods shed, a handful of wagons and a timber-framed GWR loading gauge, led to the 'Slag Siding', slightly further to the south. The Whitecroft Pin factory stands to the right.

Further along the platform (*above right*), time has obviously marched on. Other than those on special trains, passengers have not used the station since 1929; weeds march along the platform surfaces and the down track is lifted. Freight is still extant, however, judging by the mixture of steel and wooden wagons in the siding on the left and the starter signal still controlling the crossing gates. Nash & Morgan Co Ltd, coachbuilders and engineers, stand strategically placed to pick up business, but it is now unlikely to come from the railway. To the left, the goods shed looks to have received some amendments.

For once, the position is showing signs of real improvement under the aegis of the preservationists. On 30 April 2000 (*right*), although the station is no longer there in terms of platform or station buildings, the line still crosses the road and the down line has been re-laid, at least in part. Note that although the Nash & Morgan sign is still there, the firm closed shortly before this view was taken! *Crown Copyright. NMR/MJS collection/MJS*

39

Above Back at the north end of the station, on 15 April 1956, the enthusiasts' special seen on page 38 is seen again, awaiting reboarding of its passenger complement. Hauled by No 1625, the train gave its occupants a real treat, venturing (as per its headboard) deep into Severn & Wye territory. Note the dress of the day – all jackets, ties and raincoats – no T-shirts, sweaters, trainers or anoraks in those days! In the background wagons stand on what was by this time a long siding from Tufts Junction, but had originally been part of the access layout to Patent Fuel Works, the former occupiers of the Pin Manufacturing Co's site. *Hugh Ballantyne*

Opposite We take another 180-degree turn to see No 1650 about to cross the B4234 with its load of just four 16T mineral wagons, bound for Lydney Junction. Note the ubiquitous long-handled shovel and fire bucket clinging to the tank's rear brackets – but no headlamp! - and the 'Great Western & Midland Railways' sign still giving its dire warnings on the left! The ornate crossing gate bracket on the right was provided when a single structure replaced the original double gates late on in the railway's history. Note the trap points where the line becomes single.

The gates have gone, but the rails remain, as do the gateposts and the 'corner shop', still brazenly declaring its presence in bright white paint in April 2000. *F. A. Blencowe, R. K. Blencowe collection/MJS*

41

Parkend

An evocative and delightful view of 'normal' operations at Parkend: on a fine spring day in April 1959 No 3609 indulges in a little shunting before venturing into Marsh Wharf sidings to collect further stock, carefully watched by the shunter, ready for action with his pole. The fireman leans from the cab to ensure all is well before the work is restarted. Note the fire irons again on the bunker brackets, but without a shovel this time. Built in 1939 at Swindon, No 3609 spent the whole of its BR existence at Gloucester (Horton Road) shed, finally being withdrawn on 13 August 1960.

For once the view is still recognisable as being the same location. Gone are the foreground siding, gate, semaphore arm and stone abutment to the workman's hut, but otherwise relatively little has changed in this view exactly 41 years later. *Mike Esau/MJS*

We have now moved on to the station footbridge, and this is the view looking back towards Whitecroft and Lydney in 1964. The unusual triple-arm signal stands guardian over the access to and from the single 'main line', while a temporary siesta between trains is enjoyed. What had been the 'down main' is now truncated just past the pointwork by a buffer stop. The bridge, carrying a footpath from the village to the church, dates from 1900 and is by Messrs E. Finch & Co of Chepstow, replacing the original wooden structure.

The 'present' scene could almost still have been in BR days, but it is 18 May 1996 and No 4698 (renumbered from 9681 for a photographers' charter to commemorate a regular on the branch in those days) storms into the station approach with a load that would not have looked out of place 30 years earlier. *R. K. Blencowe/Graham Roose*

Another view of the enthusiasts' special of 15 April 1956, this time from the station footbridge at Parkend. Carriage doors stand wide open and No 1625 quietly simmers at the head of the train as the tour participants wander around the somewhat cramped platform area. A small knot in the foreground seems fascinated by the adjacent goods yard, while further on a group look like a marauding party bound for the signal box! The gates to the level crossing are open for the train and the semaphores give 'right away', but there is no chance of the train leaving in the immediate future! To the left of the white-painted signal box the gates are closed to the goods yard, at the point where the pre-1920 siding crossed the road, as they are beyond, to the stables outbuildings.

Three years on, in quieter mood on 10 July 1959, little seems to have changed other than the position of the level crossing and goods yard gates having been reversed; the wagon has gone from the yard siding and grass has taken a hold on the platforms. Passenger services were withdrawn in 1929 and the station 'furniture' removed soon after, leaving just the brick urinal, seen here in glorious isolation! However, as late as 1958 BR was advertising excursions and football trips from here and Whitecroft, hence the retention of the platforms.

The date of the third picture is 7 February 1971, and on the surface all appears to be drifting towards dilapidation, especially with the 'dog-leg' platform fencing. Following the closure of the branch to Coleford in 1967 the line beyond the level crossing was removed two years later, but there are tell-tale signs of hope. The site is now occupied by the new Dean Forest Railway Society, a sign has been erected on the platform on a new piece of fencing and also on the gentleman's convenience, and on the right concrete sleepers lie on the up platform ready for the restoration of the trackwork. Note how a point has been installed since the previous views. The goods shed was moved to this position in 1897, from Marsh Wharf; two of the fire buckets have gone, but remarkably one remains!; the large wooden 'box' on the yard side of the platform fencing has also gone, as have the stable buildings, replaced by a new house. The sole surviving building of Parkend's ironworks, the tall engine house to the left of the former stables, now sports an external fire escape, in keeping with its conversion to the Forestry Training School. The road crossing looks denuded without either semaphores or signal box.

Into the new century there is more progress. The platform fencing has been dispensed with, but a replica station building has been erected, complete with steps down to the old goods yard, and a new replacement signal box (ex-Mae Mawr on the TVR main line between Cardiff and Pontypridd) has appeared, ready for the time when the railway finally returns to Parkend. *MJS collection/R. M. Casserley/E. Wilmshurst/MJS*

Another panoramic view of Parkend beyond the MR signal, whose arm has accumulated a degree of unwanted coloration since the view on page 42. The gate to the yard is open in this 1964 view, but temporarily closed for access to the road both through the platforms and swinging left to the wharf sidings. Though relatively late in the day for the branch and without an actual train, the scene is still full of atmosphere and character, not least in the architectural style of the old ironworks building and, to the left, the former Station Master's house. There was originally a siding on either side of the goods shed, but the one furthest from the platform had been removed by 1920.

At platform level in the second view (*above right*) we see the station in all its early glory, with original station buildings, flower beds and bushes adorning the fence, gas lamp and, on the up platform, seating and a rudimentary waiting shelter. Undated, but probably around 1910, the ironworks have been demolished and the S&WR semaphores are 'spot-painted' in Midland style. The original William Eassie station building is the area of the middle door and the window to its right, the two 'wings' on either side having been added around 1900.

Just how much attention to detail is paid by the preservationists can be judged from the third view (*right*) around a century later, in April 2000. With replica station building and signal box, and the re-instatement of both tracks, it now only needs the fencing to be restored together with a new signal and crossing gates for the effect to be complete. *R. K. Blencowe/MJS collection/MJS*

Left A letter from the S&W&SBR's Engineer, under the auspices of the GWR at Paddington, regarding tenders for the doubling of the line between Whitecroft and Parkend.

48

Opposite In this second 'past' view from platform level, an ex-GWR railcar pauses to let its complement of passengers inspect the station in September 1950. The signalman watches from his box and a member of the train crew is in the 'six foot' checking that all is still well. The crowd, all young and middle-aged males, look to be from a charter, whereas on the right-hand platform the family group appear instead to be enjoying an afternoon stroll. Note that the signal is now Midland pattern, compared to the previous S&WR version.

The 'present' view again shows the efforts of restoration. Note how a bungalow now squats on the far hillside. *Adrian Vaughan collection/MJS*

In this view from the opposite platform, although the passengers are long gone the line is still open, evidenced by the wagons in the goods yard siding, some of the fencing uprights having obviously been recently replaced, the signal box is still operational and both running lines have been refurbished with concrete sleepers (with debris from this piled on the platform, awaiting collection). The crossing gates still have their lights intact and the ex-Midland semaphores stand guard. *MJS collection*

This is the view from the road crossing in June 1922. A Cinderford-Berkeley Road train, with its three delightfully contoured GWR four-wheeled Brake 3rd coaches at the rear and a Midland milk van behind the engine, stands in the summer sunshine, while guard and onlookers all pose for their portrait. With wheelbarrow, standard Midland lamp and the gate on the right giving access to the small goods loading bay, it is the epitome of a quiet branch-line service.

The second view was taken on the same day as that on page 49, probably around 40 years on in the mid-1960s, with the developments as mentioned previously.

Finally, the scene on 30 April 2000 shows that around another 30-40 years has reversed the previous decline and begun the period of rebuilding. *Roger Carpenter collection/MJS collection/ MJS*

Our final view of the station was taken from the signal box. No 1625 on the REC-organised 'The Severn Venturer' railtour of 15 April 1956, already seen, has now reached Parkend and gives the tour members an opportunity to detrain and take in the sights. A rare view from this angle, it shows that the goods yard siding also crosses the road, and access is controlled at both ends by single gates. Judging by the numbers on the platform and footbridge, the tour was well patronised, but one wonders how out of place the lady felt, in her fur coat, standing by the gate to the short goods yard platform! *Hugh Ballantyne*

Opposite No 3609, seen earlier on page 42, is captured at work in April 1959. Here, however, the train consists entirely of 16T mineral wagons, without the addition of vans, as seen before. The train has finished shunting duties in Marsh Wharf and is crossing the B4234 road to Ellwood to regain the main branch line, causing what looks like a Sunbeam or Hillman to wait at the crossing gates.

In the spring of 2000 the tracks still cross the road through the gate seen in front of the Peugeot 305 estate, but the tarmac is as far as they go nowadays. Beyond, much is as before to the left, with the buildings leading up to the Fountain Inn mostly still extant, but the large building seen beyond the road signpost in 1959 has gone, demolished in the 1970s and replaced by a car park. Hope springs eternal, however, within certain areas of the preservation movement that one day the railway can 're-live' its presence in Parkend. *Mike Esau/MJS*

On 8 July 1975 an unidentified Sulzer Type 2 diesel hauls a load of railway ballast forming train 8O95 for Lydney Junction. The last such train left the town at 11.40am on Friday 26 March 1976, after BR had terminated the Tilcon contract for ballast from Whitecliffe Quarry. Note that, with the run-down of the railway, the nearest crossing gate has gone, but beyond the loco a railwayman bends to lift the bolt on the sole surviving example here. The fencing certainly looks to have seen better days. Note also the prominent Forestry School building. *MJS collection*

Above The train on the previous page is crossing the main B4234 road through Parkend, having just left the wharf and crossed a side road. In this view, taken on 8 August 1966 from the brake-van of another freight train, the guard is re-opening the gates to traffic on this side road, while exchanging a few words with a passer-by. Note the frontage of the Fountain Inn on the left, and how close the tracks to the wharf come to the houses. *R. K. Blencowe*

Below Those houses, some of the oldest in Parkend, are seen again on the right as No 9619 casually shunts the wharf branch on 4 May 1964. With the sun casting shadows through the trees and hedgerow on the left towards the sturdy fencing, the easy attitude of the fireman, and the distant car with its L-plate standing on the open road, the whole has a real feeling of relaxed operations in the midst of a quiet countryside. Built in 1945 at Swindon, No 9619 spent much of its life at Hereford shed, before moving to Severn Tunnel Junction in September 1958 and suffering withdrawal on 8 August 1965. The goods shed, already seen by Parkend station, was originally sited roughly where the car stands in this view. Note the rather antiquated wooden tripod derrick crane on the 'island' loading wharf in the background, provided to serve the interchange between Milkwall and Oakwood tramways. *F. A. Blencowe, R. K. Blencowe collection*

As steam departed from ex-GWR lines, diesels took over those routes that had survived the Beeching cull. For the majority of the remaining services on the ex-S&WR route into the Forest, the BR-designed 'Teddy Bears' held sway. One such, D9555, shunts the wharf sidings on 31 March 1967, with traffic still apparently healthy judging by the number of wagons present. In the earliest days a tramroad from Milkwall arrived in Parkend at the side of this wharf, on the extreme right of this view. This tramroad was abandoned for most of its length in 1876, a stretch linking the wharf with the privately owned Oakwood tramroad being retained until the First World War. After the closure of the branch to Coleford in 1967, stone from Whitecliff Quarry was brought by road and end-tipped from the Marsh loading bank directly into 'Dogfish' hoppers, thus re-imposing an importance on to the sidings and enabling them to continue for a few more years.

Scarcely credible as the same place, the tall trees, distant horizon and houses on the right confirm the location. Despite the tracks and loading wharf still being in place as late as 1982, by 30 April 2000 landscaping has been such that virtually any evidence of the railway has been obliterated, with even the footpath to the right seemingly a natural pathway, rather than a former trackbed. *J. M. Tolson, Frank Hornby collection/MJS*

Top Another view of the area on 8 August 1966 sees D9555 easing up to a string of 16T wagons in the bright late morning summer sunshine on the main branch siding. To the left a wagon awaits loading from the road, while a few more stand by the 1868 wharf staging on the right, already loaded with coal. Having coupled its various loads, D9555 will then proceed to Lydney Junction, giving the photographer the opportunity of the brake-van picture seen on page 54. The line behind the train runs to a headshunt among the trees. Provided in 1875, on land leased from the Crown, there were proposals to extend this to join up with the branch to Coleford, which would have eliminated the need for reversal at Coleford Junction, but these came to nought. *R. K. Blencowe*

Middle Crossing the central staging, a rather unusual occupant of the siding is seen in more sunshine, this time in June 1974. Together with the coaches seen beyond it, No 4150 stands ready for the time when preservationists can work on it, while the sidings to the right are still open for the ballast. No 4150 subsequently found its way to the Severn Valley Railway. *MJS*

Bottom This view from 1971 shows the view back to the centre of Parkend, past the Fountain Inn in the centre distance. There are scotches on the rails of the two sidings on the right, to protect traffic against the falling gradient. Business has been drastically reduced since the above views and the end is now in sight, though a much reduced freight run did survive for four more years. The bright sunshine does its best to lift the spirits, but the omens are not good. *DFR collection*

Returning to the heart of Parkend, the station and signal box are seen here from a different vantage point, looking across the main road to Whitecroft towards the one climbing out of the village towards Yorkley. In this undated photograph, but probably just into the 20th century, the platform, as seen from Cinder Tips – a tip from the old ironworks, removed around 1908 – is fully occupied by a rake of ancient GWR four- and six-wheeled coaches, while the goods yard is home to a length of GWR- and MR-owned box vans. A horse-drawn cart stands by the goods shed. Note the gates, here closed to the railway on the wharf branch, the neatly painted fencing around the Station Master's garden on the right, and Parkend House, since converted to a hotel, standing proudly on the hill above the coaches. *MJS collection*

57

Back at ground level, the branch gates are again seen as we look towards The Cross, so named from the four-way crossroads in the centre of the village, created when the road in the foreground was built by the Crown, around 1903, to provide a fresh access into the Forest after the cessation of ironmaking in Parkend. When first opened up to the railway in 1868, Parkend was a labyrinth of tracks, mostly tramways, not least in this part of the town, and the end of ironworking in the town gave up this area to development and new roadways. The newsagent stands open for business in this undated view, with the signal box seen on the right and the former ironworks engine house again seen to the left.

Today only the presence of the rails still embedded in the tarmac is evidence of the previous incarnation of the area. Elsewhere, the newsagent has been replaced by a private house, trees attempt to disguise the engine house building, the signal has disappeared from the original site and a new signpost points up the hill. *MJS collection/MJS*

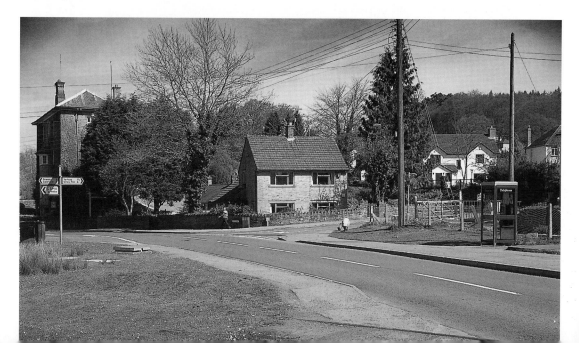

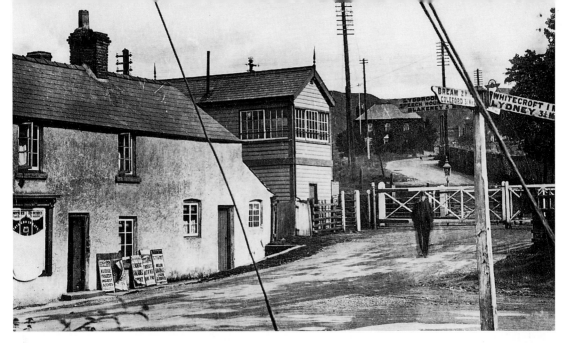

These three views are looking from The Cross up the hill towards Yorkley. In the first the signpost looks as though it is about to lose an arm, the newsagent is open, with an awning keeping out the hot 1920s summer sun, and the railway is open for the passage of a train. The hoardings outside the shop carry bold headlines, including 'Welsh Nationalist Leaders Confer', one that makes a reference to 'Teachers Salaries' and to the left one reading 'Marriage Tragedy: Inquest Scenes'!

A later view shows that the shop has been demolished, leaving just the half nearest the signal box as a cottage homestead. Traffic may well have become more of a problem by this time, as a new, higher kerb has been positioned outside this house. Fencing at the entrance to the yard behind the signal box has been renewed and an advertising board erected. In this view, the colliery pithead wheel is seen up the hill, partially concealed by the road sign in the earlier view.

Once more, the passage of time into the new century has wrought many changes. The cottage has been replaced, demolished in the 1960s and now with a sunken front garden and a kerb for pedestrians to walk along, the crossing has lost its gates after the closure of the railway, the pithead wheel has long gone, but, remarkably, the 'house on the hill' stands little altered. *MJS collection (2)/MJS*

59

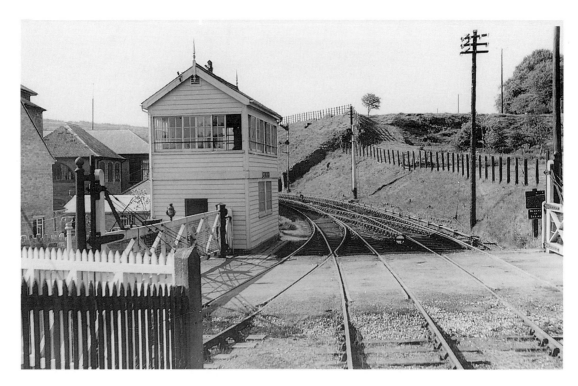

This superb view of Parkend signal box, in the late afternoon of a sunny summer's day in 1961, shows the road set for a train further into the Forest; the crossing is now protected by single gates, rather than the double version of yore. Looking as though it may well have been recently redecorated, the box, built at the same time and in the same style as those further south on the branch, the gates and the fencing all look in excellent condition.

The whole aspect of the scene is now drastically altered. Gone are the box, fence and crossing gates, as seen before, but the growth of trees and some housing development on the hillside in this view from April 2000 also make for a far more crowded feel. Note that track has been relaid by the DFR. *R. K. Blencowe/MJS*

Moving beyond the box and looking back towards the station, we see D9517 running forward from its engineering train on 20 August 1967 with what looks to be a crane within the train's consist, probably to recover equipment, as the last regular train beyond Parkend had run 16 days earlier. The gentleman on the embankment on the left, together with small boys on the platform and the signalman, all watch with interest. Note that the turnouts for the goods yard and for access between the two running lines have been lifted since the view on the previous page. Yet another of the short-lived (on BR) 'Teddy Bears', D9517 was built at Swindon in November 1964 and withdrawn less than four years later in October 1968. Sold to the NCB at Ashington Colliery, it was finally cut up in January 1984. *R. K. Blencowe*

Leaving Parkend, the line ran on to Coleford Junction, crossing the B4234 road at Travellers' Rest Crossing, named after the hostelry that once stood close by; originally The Bear, it later became The Railway Inn, before closing in 1959. Looking towards Coleford Junction, No 8745 passes over that road in April 1965 with yet another train of rail ballast, the fireman taking a breather between more arduous duties. The crossing signal box, a standard GWR design built in 1897, can just be seen above the engine's tank, while to the right the fencing once separated this line from the Parkend Royal Colliery branch. The Colliery closed in 1928, but tracks were left in situ until 1940. The bracket signal in the far distance had been the final Midland example on the branch, all signals north of that point being provided by the GWR.

Turning through 180 degrees we have one final look back at Parkend as No 8745 accelerates towards the village with its train, bound for Lydney Junction. The Forestry School building yet again dominates the townscape. *Both R. K. Blencowe*

Coleford branch

Coleford Junction, opened in July 1875, was the 'parting of the ways' immediately north of Parkend, with the branch to Coleford diverging to wend its tortuous way through the Forest to its destination. To access the branch, however, trains approaching from the south had to reverse, there being no direct south-to-west access. The branch, the extreme right-hand track is this photograph, makes a sharp turn to begin its climb above and away from the village of Parkend. In April 1959 No 3609, seen earlier shunting in and around Parkend station, here runs round its train of box vans on the up main line, prior to hauling them back into the station area. The 1908 water column, just to the right of the signal post, was invaluable, with the limited capacity of the tank engines together with the absence of other supplies between here and both Coleford and Serridge Junction.

Yes, it is the same place! The distant white house to the right gives the clue, but elsewhere the location has been transformed into a mixture of open wasteland and lorry park. Despite little actual development on the site of the old trackbed, there are no tell-tale signs betraying the past presence of iron rails. This was the view on 25 August 2001, with the once open walk/cycleway along the old trackbed, just off the picture to the right at this point, now fenced in.
Mike Esau/MJS

Above On its route to Coleford, the railway climbed up and through the western reaches of the Forest. This necessitated much twisting and turning as the track clung to the terrain, as seen in this view on 31 March 1967 as D9555 works hard up the 1 in 30/31 gradient, even with empties, away from Coleford Junction, past Point Quarry sidings. Once providing large quantities of stone, financial difficulties after the First World War saw the operations in the hands of the Receiver for many years up to final closure in 1939; beyond the locomotive it can be seen that nature is making great strides in reclaiming the quarry area. The nearby road had just as much problem with the terrain, closely mirroring the railway's route for much of the journey, as can be seen in the bottom left-hand corner. Then somewhat sparsely populated with trees, the view today is nigh on impenetrable.
J. M. Tolson, Frank Hornby collection

Opposite The end of the climb came between Milkwall and Coleford stations, at a point just beyond the road overbridge seen in the background of this view. In April 1965 No 8745 coasts down the 1 in 31 gradient past Milkwall station with yet another ballast train bound for Lydney Junction. Originally a locomotive was kept at Coleford Junction facing Coleford to cope with the exceptionally steep climb, but in the last few years of steam operation this arrangement was abandoned, hence No 8745 is facing back down the branch. The diminutive station building can be seen just above the brake-van. Though the branch to Coleford was single throughout, Milkwall had a loop to accommodate access to the Sling branch. The switch back on to the 'main line' is seen here, with the overgrown track in the centre foreground being a short headshunt.

Once more it is hard to realise that a railway ever ran here, let alone that it was once the site of a station. On 1 May 2000 only the house in the middle distance (now painted white) is a common factor. The current pathway is roughly the line of the old 'main line' on which No 8745 was running, with the Clearwell-Lane End road overbridge long gone and the road, once having to negotiate a dog-leg over the railway, now having a straight, unfettered run. It is now walkers and cyclists that must take avoiding action to prevent collision. *R. K. Blencowe/MJS*

Milkwall station is seen in its days of glory in this superb view from June 1922. A young girl rests her suitcase on the platform as she peers attentively at the timetable board on yet another Eassie S&WR building. This was obviously a time of 'TLC' for the station, as seen from its incredibly tidy appearance, the carefully tended garden area to the right of the nameboard and the station building windows looking to have been freshly painted. The period picture is completed by the 'Wright's Coal Tar Soap' advert and the Milkwall West ground frame box beyond the 1904 bridge.

By April 1959 the picture is much different. Gone is the well-cared-for look, with the platform surface and attendant 'garden' looking drab by comparison and the neat boundary fencing having given way to a more rudimentary post-and-wire affair. The large tree on the right seems to have disappeared, and so has the ground frame box. The only sign of progress is the provision of a brick building, replacing the previous wooden structure, which burned down in June 1923. Common to both views is the siding on the left trailing into the Sling branch.
Roger Carpenter collection/Mike Esau

Above Evidence of the hilly nature of this part of the Forest is provided by the railway at Milkwall. In this view the railway falls at 1 in 31 to the right, while the Sling branch, converted in 1875 from an old tramway and approaching through the gate, is climbing at 1 in 40! In this 1965 view the 1924 station building is still extant, but the platform has been the recipient of some dumping. *R. K. Blencowe*

Below With Milkwall station just visible in the distance by the base of the right-hand telegraph pole, No 3609 pauses on the Sling branch during shunting operations in April 1959. To the right of the cab stands the short-lived Milkwall Colour Works, with its short loading loop, while seen above the locomotive is the engine house of the long-extinct Easter Iron Mine. *Mike Esau*

Back at Milkwall, here is another view of No 3609 as it marshals its short train on the station loop line. The Sling branch is to the right, with the station platform just creeping into picture on the left. In early years, due to the steepness of the gradient, trains were propelled up the branch, the locomotive remaining at the Coleford Junction end.

Due to the high fencing it is impossible to faithfully replicate the earlier view; this, however, is as close as could be achieved on 1 May 2000. The only commonality is the roadway for the houses on the left, and the rough approximation of the trackbed, now surfaced for the benefit of walkers and cyclists. *Mike Esau/MJS*

Above and right At the summit just beyond Milkwall, freight trains, despite having the benefit of continuous vacuum braking, would stop to have their brakes pinned down before negotiating the severe downwards slope. In April 1965 No 8745, having obeyed the instructions on the signboard for 'ALL UP GOODS AND MINERAL TRAINS TO STOP DEAD HERE', is nearly ready for the off, having received appropriate attention.

Two years later, on 31 March 1967, the style of motive power has changed but the process is the same. D9555 stands ready as the railman approaches the last wagon. *R. K. Blencowe/J. M. Tolson, Frank Hornby collection*

Right Most railway gradient posts were angular, with a distinct 'break' between the two angles and those angles echoing the direction of the gradient. Not so the S&WR versions, which broke with convention and were a more aesthetically pleasing curve, although not mirroring the direction of slope. The severity of the climb from Coleford is denoted here by the 1 in 47, which follows the 1 in 200 from a standing start! Note in this April 1958 photograph the reversed 'Ns', the fact that in reality the gradients are both 'up', and the location of this post on the right of the top view. *T. B. Owen*

Coleford eventually had two stations, one built by the Severn & Wye and one by the GWR. A little 'over the top', possibly, for what was only a relatively small town in the Forest at the time, but some idea of the traffic expected by the S&WR can be judged from this First World War view, with the ample siding space accompanying the single platform face. The site was opened for mineral traffic in July 1875, and clearly, with this decidedly modest station, freight was expected to be more important than passengers. Seen here is the original station building, again to a design of William Eassie. To the right is a brick-built urinal (complete with appropriate 'Midland for Comfort' message!), provided in 1897 to replace an earlier Eassie-designed version. He also designed the goods shed, seen through the 1913 loading gauge.

The same view on 1 May 2000 again stretches credulity that this is in fact the same location. The site of the goods shed and sidings is now a car park, with an approximation of the trackbed leading to the town as a cycleway. *MJS collection/MJS*

During the last decade or so of operations over the Forest lines, many specials were run to enable enthusiasts to savour the delights of the railway and its surroundings. On 23 September 1950 ex-GWR railcar No W7 stands by the water column at the station while the occupants of the previously seen Birmingham Locomotive Club railtour explore the rest of the site. The substantial water tower was originally topped by a wooden tank, this iron replacement having been installed in 1895, together with those at Serridge and Lydbrook Junctions. Built by AEC/Gloucester Railway Carriage & Wagon Co Ltd in 1935, W7 was based at Worcester at the time of this view. It finally succumbed to age, changing traffic patterns and replacement by more modern traction and was withdrawn from Stourbridge shed in 1959. *P. B. Whitehouse*

71

These three views give a slightly wider perspective. The first shows yet another tour, with No 5417 ready to return 'The Severn Rambler' railtour of 1958 back down the branch, although the tour members seem more intent in gleaning every ounce of interest and pleasure from the visit. On the platform the original brick urinal still stands, but beyond are the 1921 Ladies' Waiting Room and the 1924 main station building, both built to replace the original that had burned down in 1918.

While some grass had appeared on the platform surface in 1958, it is really gaining a hold in the second view, dated 31 March 1967. D9555, already seen on its freight heading towards Coleford, has now reached its destination and undertakes shunting duties on the old coal wharf line. The goods shed in the middle distance was originally built with a 'lean-to' cover, but had lost it by this time.

One year on and it is not just the weather that lends an air of dereliction on a dull, dank and dismal 24 March 1968. Grass and weeds are now colonising the trackbed and, despite the visiting enthusiasts, there is precious little to see – certainly nothing in the way of rolling-stock. *Mike Esau/J. M. Tolson, Frank Hornby collection/T. J. Edgington*

Top and middle A final look at the station, on the occasion of yet another railtour: once more W7 is doing the honours, bringing members of the Birmingham Loco Club on a trip over the S&WR system on 22 July 1950. Again, typical British weather seems to have greeted them and the visit may not have been the highlight they were expecting. The 1924 building is seen here from a different angle; it is perhaps surprising that such expenditure was lavished on this structure at the time, in view of the fact that services were withdrawn just five years later and that the ex-GWR station, on adjacent land, was already closed and available for use.

The comments from page 70 are again pertinent here, this view looking in the opposite direction from the picture on that page. The large conifer, seen beyond W7 above, is common to both views. *Roger Carpenter collection/MJS*

Below Although the two stations in Coleford were not directly connected, there was a spur that joined the S&WR and GWR termini, paid for jointly by the two companies and in place by November 1885. It ran westwards from the former to the latter, immediately prior to reaching the former's station throat. Here the goods train hauled by No 3609, seen previously at Milkwall, runs on to the spur to access the GWR station site in April 1959. Note how open and rural the surroundings were at this date. *Mike Esau*

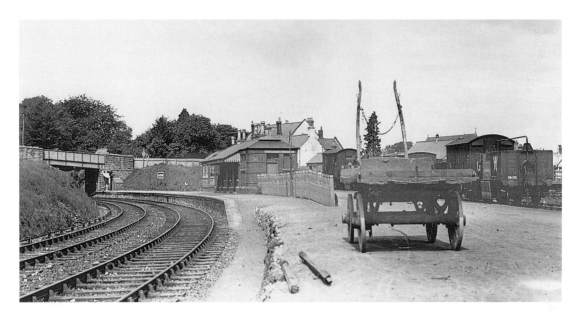

The GWR station was the terminus of a branch from Monmouth. Proclaiming its arrival with sweeping curves, altogether more grandiose buildings and spacious goods yard, almost pushing its established neighbour into the shadows, its existence was short-lived. Opened on 1 September 1883, an original intention was to have a long platform, ending opposite the S&WR station, but this was not to be. Traffic was never heavy and the station closed as early as January 1917, five and a half years before this view, but from the evidence of this photograph, complete with signal box and station name, you would be forgiven for not believing it. The line through the bridge, as far as Whitecliff Quarry, remained in use for the removal of minerals and the supply of materials, hence the wagons seen here in June 1922. The aforementioned spur gave access for this traffic to travel to Lydney via the S&WR.

By 10 July 1959 (*below left*) goods traffic is still using the area, but things have most definitely changed at the station. Gone are the starter signal, signal box and station sign, together with the platform fencing. Platform transport is still present, but now motorised as opposed to horse-drawn! Note also that the branch loop line has also been lifted.

Moving on to 8 August 1966 in the third view (*above*), the station building still looks in remarkably good condition, with the obvious changes being the lack of goods wagons and a newer motorcar standing on the platform. Motive power has arrived in the form of the ubiquitous D9555, having finished its work at Whitecliff and waiting the road to run back to Lydney, with its heavy load of just one brake-van!

As seen before in Coleford and the surrounding area, such has been the recent sweeping away of railway infrastructure that it is difficult to imagine just what there was and where. Here the house in the centre distance is a common feature, together with the conifer just to its left. Otherwise all has been obliterated in favour of the inevitable car park. *Roger Carpenter collection/H. C. Casserley/R. K. Blencowe/MJS*

Above Once more we see No 3609 and its freight train of April 1959. Taking its load of ballast empties towards Whitecliff, it pauses briefly in the GWR station at Coleford. Again, notice how, despite having been closed to passengers for over 42 years, there are still sand buckets and a porter's trolley by the station building! No sign of vandalism in those days! Such was the rivalry between companies right up to the Grouping of 1923 that the MR influence would not countenance the locals' constant cries for the GWR station to be adopted as the 'proper' facility for Coleford, an attitude that probably led to the ultimate demise of both! *Mike Esau*

Opposite This time we are looking back from the wall of the road overbridge seen in the previous views, and in June 1922 the station looks to all the world as though it is still open for business. Neat and tidy, with all the accoutrements needed for passenger operation, even the platform has not yet shown signs of neglect. Note that, even in the provision of goods shed, the GWR outshone its neighbour.

Though the site was flattened and landscaped in the making of the car park, the retention of the old goods shed provides a feature common to both views. Now preserved as a museum by Mike Rees, an ex-S&WR employee, and surrounded by other artefacts, it has at least ensured that one small part of Coleford's railway heritage survives. *Roger Carpenter collection/MJS*

Once more superficially still alive and breathing, as seen on 23 September 1950, a closer inspection of the station reveals that the signal box is closed, grass is growing on the platform and weeds are invading the tracks. However, some platform furniture still survives – thanks to the use of the station since 1918 by staff controlling the town's goods services – providing a seat for a lady who will wait in vain for a service!

Though undated, this view is suspected to be from the mid-1960s. The signal box has gone, but the station building is still in use, evidenced by the railman about to enter one of the doors, bucket in hand. In the middle distance a concrete monstrosity has been constructed to handle some of the goods traffic on offer. Elsewhere, nature is fast gaining a stranglehold. *H. C. Casserley/MJS collection*

Above As has already been seen, railtours were very popular over the ex-S&WR route in the 20 years following nationalisation. Coleford GWR was not exempt, as can be seen from this view of the REC's tour of 20 June 1964. Nos 1658 and 1664 have taken their charges to Whitecliff and are about to return them to Lydney. The complement of six brake-vans would not have been particularly comfortable, but no doubt the many heads craning out from each one would not have grumbled! *R. K. Blencowe*

Right To the left of the previous photograph can be seen the siding's platform, giving access to road vehicles for transfer of produce. The surface of this must have been not wholly forgiving, judging by this sign, positioned at the entrance to the platform on 13 May 1961. Not that many traction engines would have visited the area, surely! *R. M. Casserley*

We are now back at Coleford Junction, and an 'SLS Special' tour is seen on 13 May 1961. No 8701 pauses while No 6437, sandwiched between the coaches, gets into position for the branch, and tour members take the opportunity of stretching their legs and enjoying the spring sunshine. Note in the distance the ground-level signal box, signal bracket and road overbridge, in this view looking towards Speech House Road. Emerging from Beyer Peacock & Co Ltd in 1931, the first in a new batch of '5700' Class pannier tanks, No 8701 spent much of its life in the Hereford/Gloucester areas, finally being withdrawn on 6 April 1963 from Gloucester (Horton Road) shed.

A very similar view on 31 March 2000 shows the rudimentary footpath and cycleway and the area to the right where the trains stood in 1961. Note that some effort at recognition of the railway's past presence has been made with the signboard announcing that this was, truly, Coleford Junction. *Gerald Adams/Judi Stretton*

Top The signal box is again seen here, as No 3737 comes off the Coleford branch and runs forward with its mixed train on 2 July 1964, closely watched by signalman George Cooke, who is no doubt preparing to take the branch token from the driver. For many years, through to the 1950s, a token-catching apparatus stood opposite the box, to the left of this shot. Coming second-hand from Spythy Lane, near Swansea, the box replaced the original wooden structure that stood at a point just beyond the brake-van in this view. No 3737 was withdrawn three months later. *F. A. Blencowe*

Middle and bottom Looking towards Speech House Road and Serridge Junction, the signal gantry guarding the sidings and branch access is clearly seen on 31 March 1967. This was a BR replacement for the more elaborately designed original that stood closer to the box. A train of empty ballast hoppers stands on the single line under Naggs Head Bridge, which was provided in 1903 as part of the Crown's 'new road' through the Forest from Parkend to Mierystock. Girders for the bridge were, like the diminutive signal box, second-hand, coming from 'discarded' stock at Swindon, and the width of the span allowed for the possibility of an extended siding from Coleford Junction.

With the removal of the road bridge, the rail cutting has been infilled, with access to the other side of the road for the footpath and cycleway now being via a new path, seen on the left. Fencing guarding the road can just been seen in the 'V' between the trees, confirming this to be the same location. *J. M. Tolson, F. Hornby collection/MJS*

A last look back: seen from the road bridge in June 1963, Coleford Junction is neat, tidy and obviously well cared for, and little changed over the years except for the removal of the tablet-catcher and the provision of the new signal box and signal gantry at new positions. All the ephemera of an operating railway is here, with the exception of actual trains, but the site 'merely sleepeth' until the next arrivals. Note how the ferns are ready to reclaim their territory, however, given a chance!

The view from the site of the road bridge on 1 May 2000 gives a very different aspect. With the dismantling of the railway and removal of the road overbridge, the site is reverting to nature, with unchecked undergrowth gaining a hold from all sides. *Terry Gough/MJS*

Speech House Road and Serridge Junction

The first station into the Forest after Parkend was Speech House Road, situated literally down the road from the house that gave it its name. This is the view that a driver would have had on his approach from Parkend, with the station in the middle distance and, to the left, sidings to Wood Distillation Works and a goods shed and loading bank situated by the road, leading from the down station loop. The buffer stop marks the end of a siding from the once sizeable United Stone Firm's Howerslade loading wharf, and the open ground to its left was the route of an old tramway branch to the Cannop Chemical Works, situated across the roadway. Seen on 30 June 1964, the end of traffic some ten months earlier is becoming obvious, with the grass and weeds beginning to take hold.

Barely conceivable to being the same place, this was the view on 25 August 2001, with the car standing roughly on the line of the right-hand track and level with the point lever seen above. The road gives access to a large car park and open grassland/picnic area. *F. A. Blencowe, R. K. Blencowe collection/MJS*

Now standing on the sole platform, this June 1922 picture shows that, though isolated, the 1878-vintage station was not without a great deal of charm, including the fascinating wooden structure on the left, yet another derrick crane as seen at Parkend.

In the second picture, taken after the cessation of passenger services, a small corrugated hut has appeared by the side of the 1908 signal box, the 1888 Station Master's house, immediately beyond the crossing gates, has been redecorated, and the slot machine has disappeared from in front of the waiting room.

Into the 1950s, on 15 April 1956 a three-coach special pauses at the station for travellers to stretch their legs on a dull spring day. Some idea of the isolated nature of the station can be appreciated from this view. The 'unclimbable' fencing seems to be wearing well, but the platform surface has not been so resilient!
Roger Carpenter collection/ MJS collection/Crown copyright, NMR

By the time of this view in June 1963, when officially the site was still open for freight traffic, much of the actual station infrastructure remains, but the tracks have been truncated, with buffer stops now in place following the removal of the rails across the road in February 1962. Signal posts lie on the largely abandoned platform, obviously recognising imminent abandonment, while one of the once ubiquitous Forest sheep casually treads through what was once a pristine wooden fence. Note that the down loop has by this time been fitted with 'concrete pot' sleepers and intermittent cross stretchers (a Second World War economy measure), and the wooden panelling on the signal box indicates the original entrance and position of the external staircase.

The second, undated, view, but probably in the mid/late-1960s, shows the tracks having been recently lifted and sleepers awaiting collection. The station buildings have gone, as has the nameboard from the 1908 signal box, but the Station Master's house still stands proud, watching over the 'vandalism'.

Once more it is hard to visualise there ever having been a railway here. A sign, just past the right-hand gorse bushes, announces the site, and mock crossing gates protect walkers and cyclists as they approach the now much busier road. With the fencing on the left still, incredibly, being the original, this was the closest view to the above, with the old platform area now lost in the neighbouring undergrowth. *Terry Gough/MJS collection/MJS*

Above This view of the station at its height, seen from the other side of the tracks, shows a three-coach train about to recommence its journey towards Parkend and Lydney. Undated, but probably from around the turn of the 20th century, it bears all the hallmarks of a well-used station. The location is perhaps surprising, in view of the incredibly rural nature of the hinterland and the fact that the only building immediately in sight is the Station Master's house – after the railway had been built! – but the determining and sustaining factor was the proximity of industrial traffic, including coal, wood-derived chemical products and stone, all helped by the nearby Cannop Ponds as a water source. There are subtle differences from the 1922 view on page 84 – the station nameboard is in a different position, a gas lamp is affixed to the toilet block, the fencing is different, and the original starter signals are positioned differently before the change to accommodate GWR right-hand practice. *MJS collection*

Below From a similar vantage point on 20 June 1964 we see No 1664 with its REC special, previously seen at Coleford on page 79. While the tour members soak up the ambience of peace and serenity, the fireman takes the opportunity to rake forward some fuel for the rest of the journey. *R. K. Blencowe*

The other REC special, of 15 April 1956, already seen at previous locations, has now reached Speech House Road, and No 1625 pauses while the eager enthusiasts hurry to take in as much of the atmosphere as they can. Note the original Eassie station building on the left, and that the up signals mirror those at this end of the station.

The aforementioned station 'nameboard' can be seen here, to the left of the lone cyclist in May 2000, positioned approximately where No 1625 stood. *Hugh Ballantyne/MJS*

Above and left On 28 February 1964 the buffer stops are in place and work has started on dismantling the building, with wood from the post-1894 station extension dumped on the platform. Elsewhere the railway attempts to simulate life, with signals and sidings still in place. Coal for local merchants is dumped in the goods yard by the loading gauge.

The mock crossing gates mentioned earlier are seen to good effect here, as another cyclist prepares to negotiate the road. In this view from 1 May 2000 note how processes of nature have reworked the area, free from the hand of the railway. *F. A. Blencowe, R. K. Blencowe collection/MJS*

Right Close by the old station site is Beechenhurst Visitor Centre, one of the attractions of which is a sculpture trail, containing among the exhibits one highly appropriate idea. Taking the railway as a theme, old sleepers (paid for by an arts grant!) have been carved with motifs relevant to the Forest and the structure is laid along the trackbed, on the stretch away from the station, towards what was Serridge Junction. *Judi Stretton*

Serridge Junction was even more isolated than Speech House Road. Most views of the railway here are from ground level, but this fairly rare elevated view gives an interesting aspect on this remote junction. The line from Speech House Road on the left pierces the Forest like an arrow, with a short branch leading off it into the 1903 Crown siding, but the main interest here is No 2043 drifting down the gradient with a long train of wooden-sided wagons, full to the brim with coal from the Mierystock Colliery. Having come from the Upper Lydbrook direction, the line has skirted the line of conifers to reach the junction, an aspect not normally seen in views of the site. Note the GWR signal by the stockily built water tower and the up tablet-catcher in the left foreground. Yet another example of the numerous '2021' Class, No 2043 was built at Wolverhampton in 1898, and spent much of its time in the Gloucester/Hereford area before moving north to Birkenhead in April 1953 and being withdrawn from there on 1 January 1955.

All that now remains is a further stretch of the trackbed cycle path, seen here on 1 May 2000, peopled by Bank Holidaymakers. The gorse bush to their right is roughly where No 2043 stood, and the trackbed beyond is virtually impassable at this point. *Peter Treloar collection/MJS*

Here is yet another view of the REC 'Severn Venturer' railtour of 15 April 1956, now having reached Serridge Junction. While No 1625 is detached and taking water, the assembled throng stand and stare, or exchange comments with the guard. The layout here looks pretty extensive for this extremely isolated location, but appearances are deceptive because beyond the locomotive the two short loops end and the track quickly becomes single again for the run to Lydbrook Junction, past the conifers in the background. This route and the resulting junction was opened in August 1874 and mirrored the Coleford Junction arrangement, whereby reversal was necessary for traffic from Lydbrook to travel to Lydney. With the gradient being 1 in 40 from the Lydney direction through the junction, shunting could be a tricky manoeuvre. The substantial water tower was erected around 1896 to replace the original wooden one from 1874.

Now totally hidden by gorse and other foliage, the trackbed is lost, but with some assiduous investigation the site of the trackside hut and water tower can be found, the indentation in the embankment having not been completely obliterated. This is the view on 1 May 2000. *Hugh Ballantyne/MJS*

Most published views of Serridge Junction look back towards Speech House Road, as on the previous pages, and it is rare to be looking the other way. It is pleasing, therefore, to have this shot of W7 preparing to return to Lydney on 23 September 1950. The rarely photographed signal box is a substantial building for this outpost, important in its role of controlling both access to the Lydbrook branch and traffic to and from Cinderford (to the left in this view). Its superstructure dates from 1897 and was reclaimed from, it is thought, Lydney Junction; it had gone by 1956. The corrugated iron lamp hut, immediately to the left of the box, was provided in 1907 to assist with the lighting of signals and box in this otherwise 'dark' location. The signal gantry dated from 1903. Judging by the pile of sleepers on the left, and the very short length of turnout by the grass 'buffer stop', there has been some recent track rationalisation here.

The second very similar view dates from April 1967. Already the healing powers of nature are disguising that a railway ever existed here, and certainly give no indication of the extent of the junction layout now lifted. Just beyond the sheep, on the left of the old trackbed, stood a small platform for just a few years from 1878 to accommodate the keeper of Serridge Lodge. However, this appears to have had little patronage and soon fell into disuse. *P. B. Whitehouse/MJS collection*

BRITISH RAILWAYS
(WESTERN REGION)

STEPHENSON LOCOMOTIVE SOCIETY (MIDLAND AREA)

SEVERN AND WYE DISTRICT TOUR

SATURDAY 13th MAY 1961

	ARR.	PASS.	DEP.
	pm	pm	pm
Gloucester Central	-	-	2.15
Bullo Pill	2.33	-	2.34
Bilson Jcn.	2.50	-	2.55
Cinderford	2.57	R	3.10
Bilson Jcn.	3.12	R	3.20
Northern United Sidings	3.30	R	3.35
Bilson Jcn.	3.45	-	3.50
Bullo Pill	4.05	R	4.10
Lydney Jcn. M.L.	4.25	R	4.30
Otters Pool Jcn.	4.32	R	4.37
Lydney Jcn. (S. & W.)	4.38	-	4.40
Lydney Town	4.42	-	4.50
Parkend		4.58	
Coleford Jcn.	5.0	R	5.5
Coleford	5.17	R	5.30
Coleford Jcn.		5.43	
Speech House Rd.		5.50	
Serridge Jcn.	6.05	R	6.15
Speech House Rd.		6.30	
Coleford Jcn.		6.36	
Parkend		6.38	
Lydney Town		6.46	
Engine Shed	6.48	-	7.05
Otters Pool Jcn.	7.07	R	7.12
Lydney Jcn. M.L.	7.14	R	7.20
Gloucester Central	7.50		

Note R - Reverse

The Stephenson Locomotive Society announce:-

(1) Acceptance of The Tour Ticket implies acknowledgement that no claim is admissible in connection with this journey. Members may retain their tickets as a souvenir.

(2) Members unable to use their tickets must return them to the S.L.S. area Secretary at least one clear day before the Tour.

(3) Birmingham area members should travel by the 12.25pm Snow Hill to Gloucester Central due 1.52pm and return from Gloucester Eastgate at 8.30pm to New St. due 9.50pm. British Railways have specially agreed to a limited number of cheap day return tickets being issued at a fare of 12/6d for travel by these trains. Tickets to be booked on the day of travel at the Main Booking Office (Booking Hall) Snow Hill station and members must produce this itinerary or the 'special trip' rail ticket.

(4) A detailed map and itinerary will be handed out on the day.

In a final look at trains at the junction, we see another view of Nos 6437 and 8701 as they pause with the 'SLS Special' during its perambulations through the Forest on 13 May 1961, which included the length to Cinderford and the Coleford branch. Other than demolition trains, this was the last working on this part of the line. While railtour members have been glimpsed elsewhere in the book, this interesting and somewhat innovative shot gives a closer look at the style of clothes then worn and a fascinating comparison with how such travellers would look today. *Gerald Adams*

Lydbrook branch

Having climbed up the 1 in 40 to Serridge Junction, trains along the Lydbrook Junction branch approached Mierystock Tunnel, situated between Serridge Junction and Upper Lydbrook, on a near level 1 in 507. Just before the tunnel was reached, however, there began a sharp down gradient, at 1 in 50, which continued for virtually the whole distance to the junction. The Arthur & Edward Colliery at Mierystock was the source of much business for the S&WR and GWR/BR, but, perhaps hastened by a breach and flooding in 1949, the workings were closed in December 1959. Thankfully for the loco men, the colliery sidings were reached before the tunnel, the southern (Serridge end) portal of which is seen here on 24 March 1968. It has been a long time since trains ran through here! When the Colliery was open, some of its sidings crossed the tunnel, at right angles to the 'main line', immediately beyond the parapet. Immediately to the right of the portal, in happier times, stood a milepost showing a distance of 17¾ miles from Berkeley Road. *T. J. Edgington*

Just a mile or so down the branch from Serridge Junction, the first station reached was Upper Lydbrook. The town is squeezed in a valley between the two steep escarpments of the north-western corner of the Forest, with the railway carving a narrow ledge just above the town on the eastern side. The station was situated next to the impressive Lydbrook church, which dominates both the town and this view. To the right of the Church of the Holy Jesus, in a view from around 1910, can be seen the crossing gates, controlling passage over the then new Lydbrook- Joys Green road, the signal box and up platform, as well as the domineering topography. The scar of this new road can be seen to the right of the station, coming towards the photographer and parallel with the railway, utilising the course of an earlier footpath.

Aspects of change are obvious from this view in May 2000. While the church is now seen more clearly, with a tree partly obstructing the above view, elsewhere greenery has successfully camouflaged the railway landscape and earlier scars. *MJS collection/MJS*

Above Seen from Hangerberry Hill across the valley, effectively looking back towards the location of the previous pictures, the station layout is now more clearly seen. The main station buildings sat on the up platform, to the right of which can be seen a well-tended 'garden' bank with the station name laid out in white stones. The Station Master was awarded a £3 garden prize in 1915, and, bearing in mind clues from elsewhere in the picture, this could well be a photograph of that time. The twin tracks through the platforms run past the signal box and church, while three sidings on the down side end by the road. A railman inspects a GWR box van, while other wooden-sided wagons are of GWR, MR and private owner parentage, the latter mostly Cannop Colliery. Today not only is the far hillside covered with houses and lush growth, but also the station area has been lost – apart from a short length of retaining wall and subtle hints of what there was – under housing. *MJS collection*

Below Now 'on the ground', this is the view from the level crossing looking towards Lydbrook Junction (with Serridge Junction behind the photographer). In this attractive view, probably from around the time of the First World War, the station is obviously full of life, with that well-tended garden area, clean station buildings, notice boards and permanent way, and a porter's trolley awaiting custom. *Crown copyright, NMR*

These three views are looking back towards Serridge Junction. In the first, dated June 1922, the gates are open for the arrival of a train, but with none signalled on the up line it is to be hoped that the member of the station staff removes himself from the down tracks without delay! The proximity of the church is well seen here, as is the local terrain and the tall perch of the signal box, necessitated by the need to allow access to the platform from the road – the entrance gate can just be seen at the foot of the box. The amount and condition of the flora gives a clue to the second £3 award to the Station Master in this year!

By 1 November 1958 (*below left*) the contrast is stark! Trains now obviously no longer run and nature has begun the reclamation. The previous attractive wooden platform fencing on the right has been replaced at some time by concrete posts and wire, and the old gardener must be turning in his grave! The up loop, on the left, had become merely a siding following the end of passenger services in 1929, with Upper Lydbrook ceasing to be a block post and the whole stretch between Serridge Junction and Lydbrook Junction operating as a single section worked by train staff.

A little over 40 years later, in May 2000 (*above*), the transformation is complete. The line of the platform is hinted at by the footpath on the left, while tracks in the grass seem to echo the previous down trackbed. This is now the garden of a private house, which has been built on land from the old sidings. The church struggles to appear above the tree line on the right. *Roger Carpenter collection/R. O. Tuck/ MJS, with gratitude to the householder*

Above right and right A joint GWR & MR sign affixed to a gate at Upper Lydbrook, photographed on 1 November 1958, nearly three years after closure. One wonders whose job it was to watch those going in and out of the gate! On the same day a more common sign was seen on the signal box door, although this time Severn & Wye Joint, which is beginning to show its age! *Both R. O. Tuck*

This view of the up platform and waiting room was taken on March 1967. The tracks have gone, as have the crossing gates, replaced by post-and-wire fencing. Undergrowth is now rampant as two intrepid enthusiasts survey what remains. Note, by the side of the waiting room, the water tower that once served a urinal building, and the chimney of the 'waiting room' inserted as a 'diamond' in the corner of this end. This building had been let out to private occupiers from 1930.

A few years later and the old station building now wears a distinct air of private occupation. Sheds have been erected on both the platform and the up trackbed and a makeshift washing line has been strung up with local materials. A motorcycle sidecar sits snugly by the lower shed, with steps leading up to the platform surface, from where an Alsatian dog is obviously on the move towards the photographer. Let us hope he escaped unhurt!

Again, the rough approximation of platform level can be seen to the left, while the road can just be glimpsed through the far trees in this May 2000 view. The old trackbed is now the present house's front drive! *MJS collection (2)/MJS, with gratitude to the householder*

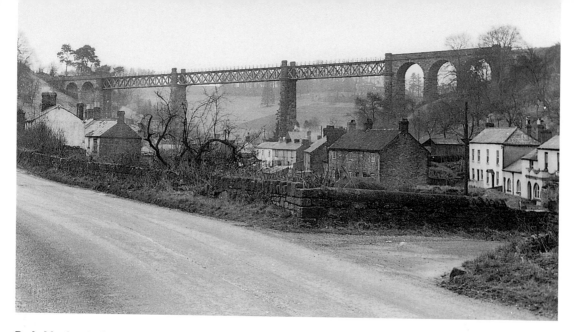

Probably the single most impressive structure on the whole of the Severn & Wye Railway system, after the ill-fated Severn Bridge, was Lydbrook Viaduct, completed on 26 August 1874, ready for the coming of the railway. Situated on the north side of Lower Lydbrook village, 90 feet above the valley and with a total span of 370 feet, it is seen here on 21 February 1964, dwarfing the nearby chapel and Forge Hammer Inn. There was no road access to the station, which opened in 1875, the only way to it being a very steep path from behind the Inn. Not surprisingly, passenger traffic was not abundant and services were withdrawn from as early as 1 April 1903!

In the spring of 1966 the end is nigh as the central span is gradually dismantled. The railway is no more and no doubt local residents felt safer if the structure was removed. It also removed an expensive maintenance liability for British Rail! The last passenger train to traverse the viaduct was a Gloucestershire Railway Society Forest of Dean railtour, on 2 June 1951, again using railcar W7, on its way to Ross-on-Wye. *F. A. Blencowe, R. K. Blencowe collection/MJS. collection*

Lydbrook Junction was where Severn & Wye met the Ross & Monmouth Railway, the latter running between the two named towns. This is the view of the last few feet of the S&WR, with the R&MR's 'main line' ahead and to the right. As seen in June 1922, facing Monmouth, the substantial water tower waits to service the branch trains reaching their destination and those on the 'main line', while to the right, as opposed to the joint nature of the S&WR, the Midland Railway is claiming sole influence. The GWR signal is for the main line, while the substantial 1907-built GWR signal box watches over both lines. Although a second platform was provided on the left, S&WR trains used the joint station platform, with the former being left to predominantly goods traffic.

By 1 November 1958 there have been many changes. The Midland signs have gone, as have the gas lamps and GWR seat; obviously, passengers were now not expected to venture this far to wait for trains! A new station nameboard has been erected and workmen's huts have mushroomed. All still appears active and the branch appears to be still open from this aspect, but the lines to the left terminate only a few feet behind the photographer.

Barely conceivable as being the same spot, this was the view on 2 May 2000, the site in commercial occupation. *Roger Carpenter collection/R. O. Tuck/MJS*

Moving past the end of the S&WR platform, the view looking across to the station buildings shows a substantial presence. In this undated view – certainly later than 1923 as the signs on the far platform proudly advertise 'LMS' – two station staff members suspiciously watch the photographer. It is likely that ex-S&WR passenger services have already ended, as the large station nameboard only faces towards the 'main line'. Elsewhere, an attractive ticket office and waiting room stands in front of the building erected in 1912 on land between the two railways by the Lydbrook Cable Works, later taken over in 1925 by Edison Swan Electric Co. On the extreme right, track is either about to be or has already been lifted, with other lengths temporarily stored on the platform.

Again undated, but almost certainly post-1960, all is dereliction in the second photograph. Gone is any pretence of 'being open for business', with a complete absence of station signs, lighting, etc, the waiting room obviously abandoned and all manner of detritus strewn about the site. Again, the length of track on the branch is deceptive. Note, however, that the large factory building beyond the waiting room has had a second storey added.

That building survives today, with its attendant house, but otherwise all evidence of the railway and its importance at this point has been obliterated. This was the scene on 2 May 2000. *MJS collection (2)/MJS*

Above To show just how far the branch still existed on 1 November 1958, this is the view of that rump of track, brutally severed without any attempt at a buffer stop. In happier times, the line ran past where the lorry is standing. *R. O. Tuck*

Below A final look at Lydbrook Junction station when it still had (some) life. Opened by the R&MR in 1873, two years before the S&WR arrived, it survived the 'newcomer' by 30 years. On Sunday 4 January 1959, the site plays host to No 6412 and an SLS Special on its outward run to Ross-on-Wye (with No 6439 on the rear), but despite the people and the activity, this is an unhappy occasion, as passenger services had been withdrawn from the 'main line' the previous day – the sun would most definitely set on the station at the end of this day! Withdrawn in 1964, No 6412 avoided the cutter's torch to be preserved, and is now more usually seen on the West Somerset Railway. *R. O. Tuck*

STEPHENSON LOCOMOTIVE SOCIETY
(MIDLAND AREA)

SPECIAL LAST TRAIN TOUR of former
ROSS and MONMOUTH RAILWAY
and former WYE VALLEY RAILWAY
(latterly Great Western Railway)

SUNDAY, 4th JANUARY, 1959

Chepstow, Tintern, Redbrook-on-Wye,
Monmouth Troy, Symonds Yat, Lydbrook
Ross, Monmouth Troy, Chepstow, Sud
Branch and Severn Tunnel Jct.

(W) (8228)
For conditions see over

Serridge Junction to Cinderford

Right and below right To all intents and purposes a decaying road bridge, or the beginning of some long-abandoned tunnel, this is in fact a brick-lined stone arch that was built around 1879 to bolster the retaining walls. These proved necessary measures, as the line ran very close at this point to a large spoil heap from Trafalgar Colliery. As seen in March 1966, a little north of Serridge Junction on the route to Cinderford, the structure, while intact and substantial enough towards the base, is beginning to look decidedly thin around the crown. The tracks have long been lifted from this stretch and, with few walkers, the fallen leaves have lain undisturbed other than by wind.

By 2 May 2000 the trackbed has been reclaimed to become a further extension of the walkway/cycleway through the Forest and, no doubt with the Health & Safety Executive in mind, the crown of the arch has been strengthened and given protection. Disruptive foliage has also been removed. *Gerald Adams/Judi Stretton*

Below A present glimpse of a past operation: a representative wagon, emblazoned in a fashion that would have been common in the Forest in yesteryear, stands among others waiting either use or restoration in the yard at Lydney Junction in May 2000. *MJS*

The remote and isolated Drybrook Road station opened for passenger services in 1875 and for a time was the closest S&WR travellers came to Cinderford! Facilities for this 'terminal' station were never lavish – a simple Eassie building, urinal and signal box – but as a station closer to Cinderford opened only three years later, there can have been few travellers from Drybrook Road thereafter. The station finally closed in 1943, still with its Nestlé vending machine in place! As with much of the S&WR, substantial freight traffic was the raison d'être and the saving grace. In its heyday the signal box, situated at the western end of the sole platform, housed 35 levers. The date of the 'past' picture is 23 August 1958 and already the remains of the station are succumbing to the encroaching grass and rhododendrons. The old Station Master's house still stands, but the access beyond the platform end is wired off. Elsewhere, lifting of the track has obviously not been that long ago, with the indentations still very visible on the ground and sleepers casually strewn around, but these latter are of no use for relaying, being in varying degrees of rot. To the right, the Mineral Loop diverted to run through the Forest to Tufts Junction, connecting mines to the S&WR and providing an alternative route south should it have been required, as well as a way of turning locomotives, as the S&WR proper did not possess turntables.

On 2 May 2000, all is tidied up and once more open for traffic, albeit foot or pedal nowadays. The sign makes plain the relevance of the site, but little else of the old railway is discernible. *Gerald Adams/ Judi Stretton*

Above The final destination of this stretch of the Severn & Wye, eventually reached in 1900 under the aegis of the joint MR/GWR administration and after much delay, was Cinderford, the first train being whistled away on 2 July. The final route approached from Drybrook Road in the west, before swinging south at the last moment to enter the station site under Valley Road overbridge. On 23 September 1950 No 1409 bustles under that bridge, up the last stretch of 1 in 164 and on to the final few yards of track into the station, with its one-coach train from Newnham. Note the antiquated wooden fixed distant signal post and arm without spectacle plate, as well as Cinderford North ground frame to the right of the train, still with its levers (for the trap point) despite the turnout and goods yard headshunt having been removed in the early 1940s! *H. C. Casserley*

Below Standing on the bridge seen above, the view towards the station complex concentrates the gaze on to the goods facilities. No 4624 looks to have a real job on its hands, shunting the collection of vans in the confines of the yard and the goods shed. The date is 8 June 1964 and while the area looks full of life, with the ex-S&WR line through Drybrook Road having been closed and lifted many years previously, this train and locomotive have reached this outpost via the old competitor – the former Forest of Dean Railway route from Bullo Pill and Newnham. *R. K. Blencowe*

Above Passenger services ceased completely at Cinderford on 3 November 1958, leaving this not insubstantial town to fall back on to less than ideal country roads. Freight between Cinderford and Serridge Junction had already come to an end, after a prolonged 'malaise', on 25 July 1949, with connections physically severed from 31 December 1951. Thus was the town isolated from the rest of the S&WR system. Towards the end, on 23 August 1958, No 1627 draws up to its coaches, having run round its short train. One of the 'new' GWR tanks, emerging from Swindon Works in BR days, on 31 August 1950, No 1627 was another locomotive to have a short 'shelf-life', being withdrawn after almost exactly 14 years on 20 July 1964, having served at three sheds, including two spells at Gloucester. With the attractively shaped trees, bright sunshine and rural aspect, the whole is a pleasing momentary interlude. *Gerald Adams*

Opposite The meandering REC railtour of 23 September 1950 is seen again; having reached the ultimate extent of the ex-S&WR route, W7 prepares to make the return journey. This could possibly have been the last train between Serridge Junction and Cinderford. The Railway Hotel stands ready beyond the station to receive thirsty customers, but those on the platform have probably not had time to indulge other than their passion for the railway on this occasion!

On the final day, 1 November 1958, the usual throng of mourners, well-wishers and interested locals and enthusiasts crowds under the small station awning, looking anxiously for their train to arrive so they can indulge their own particular last rites. A little lad sits with legs over the edge of the platform, presumably a little tired at the wait! The small brick-built structure under the lee of the trees served, in the last few years of operation, as the Station Master's office. *P. B. Whitehouse/E. Wilmshurst*

107

Looking now at the station from the other end, the Railway Hotel is behind the photographer, and the neat but somewhat cramped layout is laid out for all to see. In an undated view from around 1910, a diminutive '2021' Class saddle tank hauls into the station, to be greeted by a sizeable throng. A ticket collector stands guard by the fence, while the crowd, who seem to be dressed in their 'Sunday best', anticipate the excitement of their journey. A sister locomotive waits beyond the goods shed and there is not a weed to be seen or any item out of place.

By 25 May 1957 the site looks far more 'lived in'! With a Gloucester-bound train in the platform, awaiting the 'off', there are signs of purposeful activity in the goods yard and the station access road, with what appears to be a railway Fordson Thames 3-ton platform truck waiting to be of service. Note that since the previous photograph the garden area to the left of the platform has been cleared and grassed over and that the point rodding leading from the ground frame has been slightly re-routed.

Coming forward to 13 May 1961, yet another enthusiasts' special is visiting the area, here ready to retrace its tracks with what looks like a Diagram A43 push-pull auto-coach at the rear. The left-hand tree has grown in height over the intervening four years, now throwing a longer shadow over the platform end, where it will be noticed that the turn-out and point rodding have gone. The signal box, situated beyond the goods shed, has also gone, and the goods shed doors are unusually closed, but otherwise little else seems to have changed.

By the turn of the 21st century nothing is as it was. Standing on the far side of the road compared with the earlier pictures – to prevent staring at a brick wall! – this was the view in May 2000 from outside the old Railway Hotel. The whole site has been transformed with two recent housing developments, but the railway is not wholly ignored nor forgotten. *MJS collection/Frank Hornby/Crown copyright, NMR/MJS*

Below left A close-up of the plaque seen in the 'present' picture, which at least records that a railway once occupied this land, and recognises the names and importance of companies and individuals involved. *MJS*

Below A letter addressed to G. B. Keeling at Lydney, postmarked 1881.

Above In this undated view of Cinderford's goods yard, but probably from around 1910, a horse stands patiently waiting for its next job, harnessed to the wagon just beyond it, while another of the ubiquitous '2021' tanks shunts the nearby track. There is also an MR brake-van in the yard. The signalman looks from his box, no doubt relaxing before the next arrival and reliant on the horseshoe above his door! Note the brewery store in front of the goods shed, with empty barrels awaiting collection, no doubt from the Railway Hotel, seen beyond the station confines. The Hotel was built at the same time as the station, to greet and complement the coming of the railway. In the left distance the goods loading stage and cattle dock can be seen, with a 5-ton crane on the ground by the loco. The loading gauge seen here had previously been sited to the side of where the crane now stands. *MJS collection*

Below In this similar view on 20 June 1964, No 1658 is shunting its REC special train of brake-vans, which has reached this destination via Bullo Pill. Gone is the signal box and horse-drawn carriage, but otherwise much is as before, although appearances are a little deceptive, as passengers no longer travel from here, the station being only open for freight traffic. S&WR passenger services were withdrawn on 6 July 1929, leaving the GWR service via Newnham to cope with what human traffic there was. *Trevor Owen*

No 1627, seen earlier, here prepares to run round its train on 23 August 1958, in the last few months of service through the Forest, albeit not along ex-S&WR metals. Two modern-looking coaches would have given plenty of room for passengers at this late date in the service history!

The 'present' view of the Keelings housing development in May 2000 again shows nothing to locate this as being the same spot as above. It is to be wondered whether the occupants are aware of the heritage of their site or the relevance of its name. *Gerald Adams/MJS*

Top This delightful scene, both of ex-GWR branch line life in general and Cinderford in particular, shows an activity that has metamorphosed into an entirely different animal and has disappeared in the fashion shown here – a Royal Mail van backing up to the train to make transfer of mail and parcels, in the bright late-morning sunshine of 25 May 1957. The 'Parcels' sign, seen above the van, evidences some of the extent of the facilities originally available at the station, together with the de rigueur 'Ladies Waiting Room'! No 1623's driver casts a wary eye on the photographer, as does the besuited gentleman, presumably guarding his own luggage on the seat beside him, before boarding this train for Gloucester. The poster to the left advertises 'Camping Coaches'. *Frank Hornby*

Middle An equally attractive portrait of the station and its humble day-to-day operation is provided by this view of No 5408 and auto-trailer W206W, waiting to work the 2.45pm train to Newnham on 10 September 1955. The '54xx' tanks were derivatives of the elderly '2021s', with No 5408 seeing birth at Swindon in 1932 and death, from Gloucester, on 1 December 1956. *Hugh Ballantyne*

Bottom Ten years after national-isation and 35 years after the GWR formally absorbed all previous constituent parts, a relic of the S&WR still survived at Cinderford. Two weeks before the end of services, on 18 October 1958, a Cinderford station seat still proudly bears the carved 'S&WJR' legend. *R. O. Tuck*

These two views of the 'end' at Cinderford similarly end this section of the book. The date is 30 March 1967 and 'Teddy Bear' D9501 undertakes shunting duties, casually watched by a local coal merchant, who no doubt will not be happy at the complete disappearance of rail traffic less than five months later. Diesels had taken over from steam at the end of 1965. Note that the old brewery store has seen the addition of an end door since previous views, having been first converted in 1930 to a stable and garage, then later becoming the 'sugar shed' and 'cement shed'. The goods shed, solidly built of Forest of Dean stone with a corrugated iron roof, was ideally suited to its original purpose, but here is in the last throes of existence, with parcels traffic having gone some 18 months before this view, with the rest of freight transactions to follow before long. Likewise, D9501, built in July 1964, was withdrawn as early as in March 1968!

In the second view shunting has finished for the day, and only one 16-ton wagon needs to be moved off site, reflecting the downturn in trade. D9501 moves away from the station, bound for Gloucester, leaving us to ponder on the station's past activities and short future. *Both J. M. Tolson, Frank Hornby collection*

Preservation

Clearly, one of the first goals of any railway preservation organisation is to provide facilities for the visiting public, and the standard modus operandi is to lay sufficient track to run passenger trains. Even constricted sites, such as that of the Great Western Society at Didcot, aim at this, but for railways whose horizons are restoring at least part of old lines, this avenue is essential. Happily, over the years the new Dean Forest Railway has had the opportunity of at least a 1½-mile run, from Lydney Junction to Norchard, while keeping its sights and ambitions focused on further extension. On 29 April 2000 No 9642 receives a clear road and starts out from Lydney Junction station, the southern terminus, viewed from the signal box.

Seen from the same vantage point, another facet of essential fund-raising is seen, in the form of an ever-popular 'Drive an Engine' charter – known as 'Branch Line Experience' courses! On the same day as the previous picture, that day's 'trainees' move gently forward, about to cross the road and head for Norchard behind No 9681.

Yet another arm of fund-raising is the Gala Day, where the public are invited to attend/witness special events, such as the visit to the railway of rare and/or unusual motive power. One such was the Diesel Gala of 19 May 2001, during which several main-line diesels were on show at Lydney Junction and two Class 37s provided motive power between there and Norchard. Here No 37308 passes Lydney Junction box, forming the 16.25 service to the northern terminus. *All MJS*

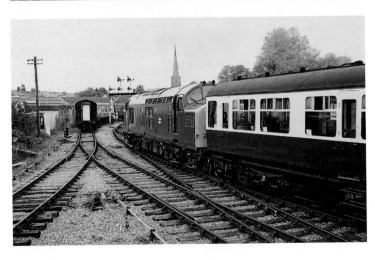

St Mary's Halt is a completely new station, with a platform rescued from Blaenrhondda. Initially opened on 8 September 1991 as Lydney Lakeside, recognising its position next to the boating lake, it provides an occasional one-platform stop for the lake, park and/or church. The simple but functional layout is seen on 30 April 2000. *MJS*

To celebrate the opening of the Halt, the railway secured a rare visit by historic locomotive No 3440 *City of Truro*. The first locomotive to break the 100mph barrier, in 1904, it is seen here relaxing on less demanding duties, pausing at Lakeside station on the opening day to allow the invited guests the opportunity of inspecting the site. At this time this was the extent of the running line from Norchard, with Lydney Junction so near and yet so far!
Hugh Ballantyne

Middle Forge is roughly halfway between Lydney and Norchard and is the location of a foot crossing over the railway. On 27 June 1990, No 9681, with its two-coach train, looks for all the world like 'the genuine article', providing a timeless view of GWR branch-line operation. Built at Swindon in May 1949, less than 18 months after nationalisation and the demise of the GWR, No 9681 operated from five different sheds – all in South Wales apart from a 4½-year stint at Oswestry – before being withdrawn on 8 August 1965. Being moved (under its own steam!) to Dai Woodham's yard at Barry Docks for scrap ironically proved to be its salvation. Bought by a group of Dean Forest Railway Society members for £3,600 in February 1975, it arrived at Norchard on 26 October of that year, where it was eventually returned to steam on 29 September 1984.

Once again on the opening day of St Mary's Halt, *City of Truro* accelerates to the crossing with one of the day's special trains. *Both Hugh Ballantyne*

Several charters have been run on the DFR over the past decade or so and one such was held on 18 May 1996. On that day No 9681, masquerading as branch regular No 4698, crosses the foot boarding at Middle Forge past one of the railway's rarest inhabitants, ex-Taff Vale Railway No 28. The sole survivor of a class of 14 built in 1897, the 0-6-2T was sold to the Longmoor Military Railway by the GWR as long ago as 1927, where it was numbered 205 and named *Gordon*. Being retained for preservation after withdrawal in 1960 and presented first to the BRB(WR), then the National Railway Museum in 1962, it eventually reached the DFR, on loan from the Museum of Wales, in 1996. Long-term aspirations are to return it to steam on the railway. *Graham Roose*

Above Although the railway's short-term target is to regain Parkend, some 3 miles or so north of Norchard, the latter has been the terminus since opening and into the 21st century. The line to Parkend rises tantalisingly above the Norchard site, seen on the right in this view, as diminutive 1952-built Peckett 0-4-0ST *Uskmouth No 1* enters with a returning shuttle of 10 September 1989, past 'Mileage Yard' box. To the right stands the railway's Wickham trolley, Type 27 No 9045. *Tom Heavyside*

Below Seven years earlier, on 24 October 1982, trains ran in much more primitive circumstances, but were appealing nevertheless, as seen in this view of No 5541 about to begin another trip with two auto-coaches. Built at Swindon in August 1928, this 2-6-2T was widely travelled before finally succumbing to dieselisation and the disappearance of its regular duties on 14 July 1962. Like many others, it found itself at Barry Docks shortly after withdrawal, where it stayed, avoiding the cutter's torch, until moving to Parkend on 11 October 1972. Restoration to steam was achieved on 29 November 1975. *Tom Heavyside*

By the turn of the new century another platform had been provided at Norchard, a few yards beyond the brake-van in the upper view opposite. This latest arrangement gives a far greater operating flexibility, with access to the shop and museum for the public and run-round facilities for the locos. On 1 May 2000 No 9642 approaches the station, about to give up the branch line token to the signalman, as it brings the 15.55 ex-Lydney Junction service to its destination. Sister to No 9681, it emerged from Swindon in 1946 and served at various sheds before ending up at old Oak Common on 24 August 1964, from where it was withdrawn three months later. Leading something of a charmed life at scrap merchant Hayes of Bridgend then Jones Brothers of Maesteg, No 9642 subsequently found its way to the Swansea Vale Railway, before coming to the DFR on 18 April 1998.

The new layout also gives waiting travellers a closer view of the engine shed and works yard. On the same day, one of the railway's two Class 108 diesel multiple unit sets, ex-Eastern Region E50619 (of 1958) and Midland M56492 (1960), stand in the yard, not required for the day. *Both MJS*

While the vast majority of the visiting public prefer to see and travel behind steam engines, a mixture of steam and diesel does have the potential of pleasing a greater percentage of those visitors and also shows both the development and variety of past railway practice. During the previously mentioned Diesel Gala of 19 May 2001, both sit happily side by side in Norchard yard, with home-based *Uskmouth No 1* and No 5541 in company with visiting No 37029.

To the left of the above view, visitors can inspect the workshops and yard. Inside in May 2000 was No 5521, partially stripped to receive remedial attention. New from Swindon in 1927, it was, like sister No 5541, widely travelled, finally 'coming to rest' at Laira shed on 21 April 1962. Yet another locomotive to dice with death at Barry Docks, its stay was from 1962 until September 1975, when it was initially sold for use on the West Somerset Railway. It was sold on to Bill and Dick Parker, under whose ownership it has seen some restoration at a number of sites. A year after this view, on 12 July 2001, the locomotive was moved to nearby Bream, where, in Bill Parker's own 'Swindon Workshops', final restoration will be achieved. *Tammy Stretton/MJS*

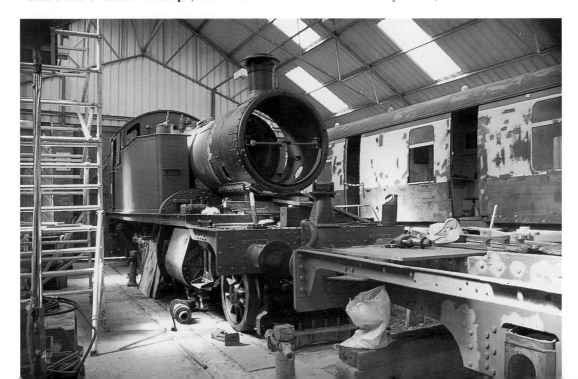

In a final view of the current terminus at Norchard, taken from the engine yard, we see No 9642 standing in the station waiting to take another load of passengers to Lydney Junction and back, in May 2000. To the right is the 'Royal Forester' dining set. *MJS*

A glimpse of the future? When services eventually return to Parkend, trains will avoid Norchard and climb past on a higher level, as described earlier. On 25 April 1982, 1953-built Hunslet 0-6-0ST No 3806, here as No 4 *G. B. Keeling*, looks intent on being ahead of the game as it stands on that higher ground during a test steaming. Named in 1981 by the Rev Wilbert Awdry, it was subsequently renamed *Wilbert* to commemorate him. The present run into Norchard can be seen in the distance, between the locomotive and left-hand tree. *Tom Heavyside*

While the passenger services are the glamorous face of railway preservation, infrastructure preparation and maintenance is largely unsung, but is an essential ingredient of a successful operation. On 30 April 2000, in furtherance of that push for Parkend, one of the DFR's ex-BR 08 shunters, No 13308, is coupled to ex-Reading crane No 81548 to clear old redundant sleepers near Whitecroft. Built at BR's Darlington Works in May 1956 and renumbered D3308 in October 1958 under the 1955 Modernisation scheme, the shunter started life at King's Cross shed and ended up at Gloucester, from where it was withdrawn in March 1984. Restored in part of the old Swindon Works, it came to the DFR on 9 December 1992.

On the other side of the road crossing at Whitecroft, on the final leg to Parkend, No 9681 again assumes the persona of a sister loco, this time No 3775, as it runs towards that next goal with a freight charter. *MJS/Mike Esau*

Right With services not yet able to resume to Parkend, the only chance of seeing movement there is either a DFR working party or a special charter. One of the latter is seen on 18 May 1996, when No 9681 (here alias No 4698) runs into the station approach with a 'ballast' train. *Hugh Ballantyne*

Below A 'bridge' too far? On 6 June 1995 what appears to be No 1458 of 89A Shrewsbury shed – but in reality is No 1466 from the GWS at Didcot – seems to be about to retrace the Marsh wharf branch at Parkend, but nearly 20 years after the last train ran from here, this is as far as this train, another special charter, can go! It does, however, create a wonderful image and a tantalising glimpse of what might have been. *Mike Esau*

A final look at steam on the Dean Forest Railway and a view that hopefully will become far less rare in the near future. On 28 March 1976, in the early days of the DFR, No 5541 looks to be undertaking shunting movements at the side of Parkend station, but is in fact undergoing a steam test following years of 'open-air' restoration. From 25 August 2001, on normal steam days, a DMU shuttle runs to just short of Tufts Bridge – Parkend is next! *Tom Heavyside*

GAZETTEER

Berkeley Road-Lydney Junction

Under an Act of Parliament of 18 July 1872, the Severn Bridge Railway was to construct a line from Lydney to Sharpness on the other side of the River Severn, with the Midland Railway to also construct a link to Sharpness from its existing site at Berkeley Road, on the Birmingham to Bristol main line. Though not sponsored by the S&WR, George William Keeling (Engineer of the S&WR and son of George Baker Keeling, who had done much to salvage and steer the S&WR since 1847) was appointed Engineer of the new railway. The MR, together with contributions from the S&WR and forest mine-owners, provided much of the necessary finance, and construction of the bridge over the Severn was begun in 1875, coincidentally the same year as passenger services started on the S&WR. By 1878 the S&WR – never financially flush – was experiencing yet more difficulties, so, when additional funding was required to complete the Severn Bridge, the Midland stepped in on the condition that it acquired running rights over the S&WR. This was agreed, on the basis that in turn the S&WR could run to Berkeley Road. Thus, from 1879 S&WR trains ran between Berkeley Road and Lydney, over the bridge and along a track separate to but parallel with the South Wales main line. Mileages were amended at this time to reflect the change, by adding 8 miles to the previous logs, which began at Lydney.

Initial services were for seven trains in each direction, with two of the down trains running through to Lydbrook Junction, one to Cinderford with a connecting service to Coleford, and the remainder only travelling as far as Lydney Junction. A new station was built at the latter, to replace the existing S&WR site. From 1894, after a protracted period of hardship for the Forest and S&WR and 'devious' competition by the GWR, a joint MR/GWR administration took over, with the former effectively operating from Berkeley Road to Lydney and the GWR from there into the Forest. This continued after the 1923 Grouping as an LMS/GWR partnership, with around eight trains per day each way. Thereafter, the joint railway operated services largely forgotten and ignored by the outside world, until the night of 25 October 1960, when Britain's third longest railway bridge was struck by two oil tankers (the *Arkendale* and the *Wastdale*) in thick fog. Two of the spans of the bridge collapsed into the river, ending at a stroke 81 years of trains between Lydney and Berkeley! Formal closure did not come until 2 November 1964, the date passenger services ceased between Berkeley Road and Sharpness. This left just a stub of the branch, to Sharpness, to continue for freight.

Lydney Junction-Parkend

Eventually forming the central stretch of the whole route from Berkeley Road to Lydbrook Junction, this 4-mile section was the first to open, in 1868. The Lydney Junction MR/GWR joint station opened in 1879, on the curve connecting the old S&WR route from the Forest to the Severn Bridge. It replaced the original S&WR facility, situated end on to the South Wales Chepstow-Gloucester main line, which then became subsumed into the enlarged Junction sidings layout. In 1899 157 men were employed at the Junction, presumably including those based at the engine shed. Originally built around 1865 for the S&WR, this latter facility was rebuilt and enlarged in 1876, 1891 and again in 1892, to accommodate increases in traffic, manpower and size of locomotives.

The line from here to Parkend was laid alongside existing tramways and opened for traffic –

Welsh coke shipped to the ironworks at the northern terminus – on 19 April 1869, hauled by the S&WR's new locomotive, broad gauge 0-6-0ST *Robin Hood*. Passenger services began on 23 September 1875, after conversion to standard gauge, but were overtaken by improving road services throughout the Forest, compounded by many of the locations being so isolated. Such services were therefore withdrawn from the whole of the S&WR system north of Lydney Town on 6 July 1929. Freight traffic, initially from/to the ironworks at Parkend and Parkend, Princess Royal and Norchard collieries, continued, with quarry and coal traffic especially important. This too, however, finally succumbed to both changing social habits and the expenses of running a declining industry. The last 'regular' freight ran on 7 May 1976, when all remaining wagons at Parkend were transferred to Lydney yard. Thereafter the line remained in situ but not officially closed, in the hope of open-cast coal traffic. This, however, never materialised. BR ran an engine and brake-van over the line at regular intervals to keep it 'open' – this also acted as a crew training turn. The line was finally turned over to the DFR in late 1980.

Parkend-Serridge Junction

Like the section above, this stretch was opened in 1868 as a broad gauge railway alongside the tramway, initially to connect with the Wimberry Colliery, near Speech House, just short of what became Serridge Junction. Speech House Hill Colliery was also nearby. Speech House Road station, 2½ miles from Parkend, opened with the commencement of passenger services on the S&WR in 1875. A single platform and isolated, traffic was never heavy and closure to passengers came with the rest of the railway in 1929. The two collieries were finished as independent concerns by 1906 and became, under various transactions, part of Cannop Colliery, a syndicate formed of Northumberland businessmen! With varying fortunes, mining continued until, under the management of the NCB, final closure came in September 1960, with the very last traffic leaving the sidings on 21 November.

Serridge Junction became a junction in 1874, when the line to Lydbrook Junction opened in August of that year. An trailing junction from the Parkend direction, it entailed an awkward reversal for trains on steeply inclined track. It was never blessed with a station, being merely the point where goods and mineral traffic from Lydbrook – and initially also passenger services to Cinderford – met the 'direct' line from Lydney. A remote railway outpost, it was overseen by an isolated signal box. Passenger services again ceased over this line in 1929 and freight northwards to Drybrook Road disappeared from 31 December 1950. Southwards to Wimberry Junction and westwards to Mierystock Sidings ceased after 31 July 1956, although the track was left in situ.

Serridge Junction-Cinderford

From Serridge Junction the line initially ran north-eastwards, before arcing to travel to the east, past Trafalgar Colliery, arriving at Drybrook Road in June 1872, as part of the Mineral Loop from Tufts Junction. One mile from Serridge Junction, it became the effective S&WR station for Cinderford, but at 1½ miles from the town and again isolated, it was hardly ideal and there were many complaints from the locals. When S&WR passenger services were introduced in 1875, one train a day travelled from Drybrook Road to Lydbrook; its other importance was that other services from Lydbrook, southwards towards Parkend, were not allowed to reverse at Serridge Junction, but instead were forced to run to Drybrook Road then return up the line after the locomotive had run round its train! After the brief use of a halt slightly closer to Cinderford, called Bilson Platform, a new station was opened nearer the town on 29 August 1878. Still not ideal, situated on a spur at Bilson Junction to a line going away from the town, road access was far from satisfactory. As part of the takeover of the S&WR by the MR/GWR partnership in 1894, a new Cinderford station was to be built much closer to the heart of the town and this was eventually achieved on 2 July 1900. This new station was then the recipient of passenger and freight traffic from the S&WR and the more direct GWR route from Newnham.

Together with the rest of the S&WR, passenger trains at Drybrook Road and into the new Cinderford station ended in 1929 – although freight facilities continued at the former until 30 September 1943. The clamping out of use of the short spur from Laymoor Junction to Cinderford Junction and the stretch from Serridge Junction to Drybrook Road on 31 December 1950 effectively killed off any hope of through services of any kind along the old S&WR route – although traffic had actually ceased some time earlier. Formal closure between Serridge Junction and Cinderford Junction came on 9 December 1951, although the part between Drybrook Road and Laymoor Junction was used by the military until 16 June 1953. Passenger services over the ex-GWR route ended on 3 November 1958, with the last freight from Cinderford station running on 3 August 1967 and formal closure 11 days later.

Serridge Junction-Lydbrook Junction

Authorised in 1870, the line from Lydbrook Junction was opened to Serridge Junction on 26 August 1874. As already seen, passenger services over the line commenced on 23 September 1875. Its conception followed the desire to move iron-ore from local quarries to customers outside the Forest, and there were many sidings along the route for the purpose. The first station was at Upper Lydbrook, some 2½ miles from Serridge Junction. Opening with the commencement of passenger services in 1875, it was a relatively important place on the branch, being a station with two platforms, a passing loop and a respectably sized goods yard, and close to two mines. As with the rest of the S&WR, passenger trains ceased from 1929 and regular freight services between here and Lydbrook Junction ended on 1 January 1953.

Lower Lydbrook, perched high above the village of the same name, just three-quarters mile further on, was also opened in 1875, but public access was tortuous, up a steep footpath from the village with no vehicular access at all. Traffic was never heavy and as early as the turn of 1903,it had become an unstaffed halt, finally closing on April Fool's Day of that year! Lydbrook Junction, a little over 4 miles from Serridge Junction and 20¾ as measured from Berkeley Road, became a junction – with the Ross & Monmouth Railway's line, opened on 3 August 1873 – with the arrival of that first train over the S&WR branch on 23 September 1875. Termination of service details on the branch are given above.

Coleford Junction-Coleford

Authorised in July 1872 and constructed following much of the route of the Parkend-Milkwall tramway, with steep gradients and many reverse curves, before taking a virtually direct line from Milkwall into Coleford, the branch was opened for goods traffic on 19 July 1875 and passengers nearly six months later, on 9 December. Throughout its life the punishing 1 in 30/31 gradients were severe restrictions on the operating of the branch, with, initially, locomotives being marshalled at the Coleford Junction end to prevent dangerous runaways!

Milkwall was the only intermediate station on the branch, half a mile or so from the village it purported to serve. Traffic was, as with many other stations on the S&WR system, never heavy and passenger facilities were withdrawn in concert with its contemporaries in 1929. The station was the junction for the Sling branch, which brought some freight business to the area well into the 1960s, with the last train being for scrap in July 1965.

The S&WR station at Coleford was always an unprepossessing affair compared to its nearby GWR neighbour, which arrived in more confident style in September 1883. Initially there was no physical contact between the two, although they were adjacent, but a connecting line was eventually provided, and after the S&WR station closed to passengers in 1929, many of the goods staff transferred to the relatively more opulent facilities at the rival building, with all freight traffic then being handled from that site. The GWR passenger services were withdrawn even before the S&WR ones, with that railway's branch closing in 1917, leaving the S&WR goods traffic to serve the town until the end on 2 October 1967.

INDEX OF LOCATIONS